CW00327425

MILLER'S
Antiques Checklist
PORCELAIN

Consultant: Gordon Lang

General Editors:
Judith and Martin Miller

MILLER'S

MILLER'S ANTIQUES CHECKLIST: PORCELAIN

Consultant: Gordon Lang

First published in Great Britain in 1991
by Miller's, an imprint of Octopus Publishing Group Ltd.
This edition published in 2000 by Chancellor Press,
an imprint of Bounty Books, a division of
Octopus Publishing Group Ltd,
2–4 Heron Quays, London, E14 4JP

Miller's is a registered trademark of Octopus Publishing Group Ltd.

Series Editor	Frances Gertler
Editor	James Chambers
Senior Art Editor	Eljay Crompton
Art Editor	Al White
Assistant Art Editors	Richard Scott, Eng Lim Khaw
Illustrator	Simon Miller
Editorial Assistant	Katie Martin-Doyle
Typesetter	Kerri Hinchon for Evolution
Production	Sarah Schuman

American consultant: Nicholas Dawes

©1991 Octopus Publishing Group Ltd.
Reprinted 1995, 1996, 1998
This edition published 2000

A CIP catalogue record for this book is available
from the British Library

ISBN 0 75370 317 3

No part of this work may be reproduced or utilized in any form or
by any means, electronic or mechanical, including photocopying,
recording or by any information storage and retrieval system,
without the prior written permission of the publishers.

The publishers will be grateful for any information that will assist
them in keeping further editions up to date. Although all reasonable
care has been taken in the preparation of this book, neither the
publishers nor the compilers accept any liability for any consequences
arising from the use thereof, or the information contained herein.

Set in Caslon 540, Caslon 224 bold and Caslon 3
Produced by Toppan (HK) Ltd
Printed in China

Jacket: *A Worcester hexagonal vase decorated with the typical scale-blue
ground and "fancy-birds" decoration in reserved panels, c.1765-72*

CONTENTS

AMERICAN PORCELAIN

COPIES AND FAKES

MARKS 176

GLOSSARY 177

BIBLIOGRAPHY 183

INDEX 185

ACKNOWLEDGMENTS 192

HOW TO USE THIS BOOK

When I first started collecting antiques although there were many informative books on the subject I still felt hesitant when it came to actually buying an antique. What I really wanted to do was to interrogate the piece – to find out what it was and whether it was genuine.

The *Porcelain Checklist* will show you how to assess a piece as an expert would, and provides checklists of questions you should ask before making a purchase. The answer to most (if not all) of the questions should be "yes", but there are always exceptions to the rule: if in doubt, seek expert guidance.

The book is divided by continent, and within each continent by country and factory. At the front of the book is a special section on how to look at and handle porcelain, and on the colours used by the principal factories. At the back of the book is a glossary and bibliography. The book also has a chapter on copies and fakes – some of which are collectable in their own right – and porcelain marks.

Treat the book as a knowledgeable companion, and soon you will find that antique collecting is a matter of knowing the right questions to ask.

JUDITH MILLER

Each double-page spread looks at the work of an individual factory.

The first page shows a carefully chosen representative item of a type that can usually be found in antiques stores or auction houses (rather than only in museums).

The caption gives the date and dimensions of the piece shown, and a code for the price range of this type of article.

A checklist of questions gives you the key to recognizing, dating and authenticating antique pieces of the type shown.

CHELSEA 1: 17

A Chelsea salt, modelled as a crayfish, from a silver origin c.1745; width 5in/12.7cm; value code

Identification checklist for Chelsea por
1. Is the porcelain soft-paste?
2. Are there any black "pinholes" on th
3. Have the bases of hollow vessels and ground down?
4. Is the piece shaped like silverware or
5. Are the form and the decoration deriv
6. Is the palette predominantly puce, bl greenish turquoise (especially 1749-52
7. If a figure, is it hollow, and smooth i
8. If a vessel, does the piece have choc
9. Is it marked (see *opposite*)?

Chelsea (1745-69)
The only 18thC English factory to concentrate entirely on luxury porcelain was founded in London in 1745 by Nicholas Sprimont, a Huguenot silversmith from Liège. Because he was aiming his products at "the Quality and Gentry", he opened his factory in Chelsea, close to the fashionable Ranelagh pleasure gardens. The history of the factory divides into four periods, each identified by a different mark.

Incised-triangle, 1745-49
The mark for the earliest period is an incised triangle, although a few of the first pieces are marked with a trident piercing a crown in

underglaze
The smal produced o predominar beakers, te Sprimont w influence c into Englis undulating of these wa designs he silver.
• Many wa the main p nocks, shel decorative trailing veg
• Crayfish Worcester Bristol fact

112

A list is provided of the factory's principal products.

VALUE CODES
Throughout this book, the caption of the piece in the main picture is followed by a letter that corresponds to the approximate value (at the time of printing) of that piece. The values should be used only as a general guide. The dollar/sterling conversion has been made at a rate of £1=US $1.50; in the event of a change in rate, adjust the dollar value accordingly.

Marks, signatures and serial numbers are explained.

The second page shows you what details to look for.

Further photographs and/or line drawings show:
* items in a different style by the same factory (or individual craftsman)
* common variations on the piece shown in the main picture
* similar wares by other craftsmen or factories
* the range of shapes or decorative motifs associated with a particular factory or period
* the styles and idiosyncrasies of the factory's leading potters, modellers and decorators.

Useful background information is provided about the factory.

EUROPEAN

Incised-triangle paste
The earliest Chelsea soft-paste is glassy and creamy, like early St Cloud or Mennecy.
* The milk-white glaze is often unevenly applied. It contains a few black "pinholes", and there is sometimes a narrow, unglazed margin around the base of the piece.

Raised-anchor, 1749-52
In 1749 Sprimont moved his factory to new premises and introduced a new mark, an anchor moulded in shallow relief on a small oval pad. With financial backing from Sir Everard Fawkener, who was secretary to the King's brother, the Duke of Cumberland, Chelsea embarked on a brief period of expansion which was to be its most successful both commercially and artistically.

With the help of Sir Everard, who was a friend of the British ambassador in Saxony, the Chelsea modellers borrowed and copied a large number of Meissen figures. Although most of them were later painted – the best of them, like these goats, in the workshop of William Duesbury (see p.151).
* In addition, the Flemish modeller Joseph Willems modelled a fine series of birds based on the engravings of George Edwards, and also a range of fairly large theatrical, Oriental and contemporary figures based on the engravings of Ravenet, Cochin, Balechou, Aveline and Callot.

Although the silverware shapes continued, the main influence at Chelsea during the raised-anchor period was Meissen. Many of the Kakiemon shapes and patterns which Meissen had been reproducing since the 1730s were copied in the new soft-paste porcelain and decorated using an autumnal palette of puce, brown and greenish turquoise, similar to the palette at Vincennes. On some pieces, such as this chrysanthemum bowl, the Japanese shape is decorated in a European pattern.
* As on most raised-anchor vessels, the rim of the bowl is edged in dark chocolate brown. This was added in imitation of Meissen's version of the Kakiemon style, but on the original the decoration had a practical purpose – the Japanese vessels were rimmed in iron glaze to stop them chipping.
* The most original decorations on raised-anchor wares are the scenes from *Aesop's Fables*, which continued to be used in the red-anchor period and were probably all painted by O'Neale, an artist who later worked at Worcester.

Raised-anchor paste
The raised-anchor paste is less glassy than incised-triangle paste and the milky glaze has a duller *faïence*.
* The bases on many wares are covered in an uneven glaze with numerous "pinholes" and a few grey spots in the surface.
* Some wares were very thickly potted, which often made them warp during firing.

Like Japanese porcelain, Chelsea wares were fired on top of three little porcelain spurs, which were usually on the footrim but occasionally on the base. As this allowed glaze to dribble over the foot, the footrims of hollow vessels and dishes were usually ground down after firing.

The most common shapes and decorative designs are discussed, as well as the shapes and designs that are unique to the factory.

The codes are as follows:

A £25,000+ ($37,500+)
B £15-25,000 ($22,500-37,500)
C £10-15,000 ($15-22,500)
D £5-10,000 ($7,500-15,000)

E £2-5,000 ($3-7,500)
F £1-2,000 ($1,500-3,000)
G £500-1,000 ($750-1,500)
H under £500 (under £750)

INTRODUCTION

Collecting Porcelain

The practice of collecting porcelain in a systematic manner is probably a relatively late phenomenon in the Western world, although various pieces are included in the inventories of great and noble families in France and Italy during the 14th and 15th centuries – for example, a shallow porcelain bowl is recorded among the treasures of Louis, Duke of Anjou in 1379-80, probably because it was rare and costly rather than as part of a formal collection.

It was almost certainly not until the 17th century, when porcelain was available in far greater quantities than ever, especially in Europe, that anything resembling a system or classification could be applied to the collecting of porcelain. However, it was an enthusiasm that caught on quickly: the early 18th-century English novelist and essayist Daniel Defoe referred to what he regarded as Queen Mary's excessive mania for collecting china.

Since then, collectors have become increasingly sophisticated in their approach to porcelain-collecting, especially in the last generation or so. Within the space of twenty years, an enormous number of specialized books, monographs and papers have helped to illuminate this vast topic. Ongoing excavations and research force constant reappraisal, especially with regard to attribution. In the 1960s attributions were generally looser – for example, the terms "Rockingham" and "Coalport" were freely applied to anything encrusted with flowers or even Neo-rococo in style. The same was true of many porcelains then classified as "Liverpool" but which in the light of recent research have today been identified as Vauxhall or Limehouse. However, although it is possible to be fairly precise in attributing most porcelain, there are still many under-researched areas in which an astute and assiduous amateur could discover pieces of interest at undervalued prices.

Whether you are buying porcelain for its decorative appeal, or its rarity or even for its association with a historical person or event, the choice is very broad. Some collectors concentrate on a specific factory, period, type of object or decorative theme. It is essential to gain as much experience as possible from handling and examining pieces known to be genuine. Time spent at museums to become familiar with the best examples is a good foundation, but it is equally, if not more important to actually handle the porcelain pieces themselves. The best places to do this are the auction houses and stores of specialist dealers. Bear in mind that the more research you have done, and the more interest you manifest, the more experts will be inclined to discuss their subject and their stock.

Marks

Although many people look for a mark first as a way of identifying a piece of porcelain, marks can be deceptive – for example, a good number of factories copied the marks of more fashionable porcelains, especially those of Meissen and Sèvres. Therefore, more emphasis has been placed in this book on teaching collectors how to identify a piece through other, more reliable signs, such as the composition of the porcelain body, known as the paste, the type of glaze, the style of the piece, and so on. The mark should then be used merely as confirmation of what has been deduced by looking at these other "clues".

The market
Potential buyers should find out what is currently enjoying a boom and what is in the doldrums. At the moment there is generally greater interest in wares than in figures, although there are a number of spectacular exceptions such as Capodimonte (see pp.154-5) and Nymphenburg (see pp.76-7). However, buying what is unfashionable now may well prove in time to have been a good investment. Rare examples of any type of porcelain will always command high prices, whereas more mundane specimens are subject to greater fluctuations in the market. Condition is very important: while rare or important pieces no longer in perfect condition can still command enormous sums, damaged run-of-the-mill porcelains should be avoided, except perhaps as study pieces.

This book
The method used throughout this book is founded in the visual analysis of porcelain; the same systematic procedure as that employed by a forensic scientist looking for clues, and it requires the same patience and powers of observation. The book concentrates on the work of all the important kiln sites and European and American porcelains, and in each case on the period or wares of greatest interest to collectors: even the major factories sometimes produced wares that are not highly collectable. A special section at the back of the book also looks at copies and fakes and distinguishes between copies that have over time become collectable in their own right and out-and-out frauds. However, remember that making mistakes is all part of the learning process – even top dealers have sometimes been fooled. With time, you will acquire the experience and confidence to make informed and sound judgements and with that will come the joy and satisfaction of collecting porcelain.

GORDON LANG

HOW TO LOOK AT PORCELAIN

Paste

The first step in identifying a piece of porcelain is to examine the paste, that is the unglazed porcelain body, which can usually be seen on the base. The only time when this is not possible is when the piece has been glazed overall, like the Bow flatwares, which stood on tiny stilts in the kiln. But on these rare occasions the overall glaze is itself a clue to the piece's identity. The first question to ask when examining a piece is whether the paste looks like sand or like icing (confectioner's) sugar. In other words, is it granular, or smooth, or some stage in between? If it tends towards the granular, it is more likely to be soft-paste; if it tends towards the smooth, it is more likely to be hard-paste. There are of course exceptions, which can only be learned with experience, and there are also some pieces which are deceptive. For example, the bases on some Chelsea wares are ground away, which makes the unglazed areas look very smooth, although in fact the porcelain is a granular soft-paste.

Soft-paste was developed in Italy under the patronage of the Medicis at the end of the 16thC. It scratches and chips more easily than hard-paste, and the chips, which look like broken biscuit, are very different from the smooth hard-paste chips.

Hard-paste is the formula for Chinese porcelain, which was first made in Europe at Meissen, in Saxony, at the beginning of the 18thC. The essential ingredients are two types of decomposed granite, kaolin (china clay) and petuntse (china stone), which fuse to the hard consistency of glass in the high temperatures of the kiln.

Having decided whether the porcelain is hard- or soft-paste, there is one last question to be asked about the paste. Can the factory be identified by the colour? For example, is the paste pure white, like *blanc de Chine*, is it a dark colour, like the grey paste of Doccia, or has oxidization in the firing stained it with tiny brown patches, like Lowestoft?

Glaze

In studying the glaze, we are also

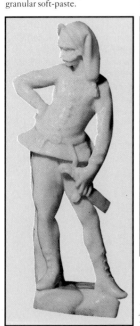

The thick glaze on the soft-paste Capodimonte figure, left, has obscured most of the detail, while the thin-glazed hard-paste Nymphenburg figure above looks as crisp as a carving.

looking at different stages between extremes: is it either dull or matt on the one hand, or alternatively, smooth or glassy? Is it transparent or is it opaque? Is it thick or thin? The glaze can be as much a clue to a piece's origin as the paste. For example, Mennecy and St Cloud used a glaze that was very transparent, while Doccia and Chantilly used an opaque glaze with tin in the formula, probably in order to hide blemishes in the paste. On early Worcester the glaze is very thin, while on gold-anchor Chelsea it is exceptionally thick. In general the glazes on soft-pastes are thick and tend to conceal the details. As a result, soft-paste figures often look like melting ice and most of them suffer in comparison with their thin-glazed, hard-paste counterparts.

If a glaze contracts more than the paste as it cools down after firing, it breaks into a network of irregular cracks, known as crackle. As this tended to happen at some factories more than at others, it can be another clue to the identity of a piece. For example, it is found on the thick-glazed, gold-anchor Chelsea wares and on several other soft-pastes, and also on early Chinese stoneware, where it was often produced to obtain a decorative effect.

Decoration

The style and technique of the decoration are often important evidence of a piece's origin. Decoration can be incised or moulded, printed or painted; and it can be applied under the glaze or over the glaze, which can usually be felt with the fingers. But the most useful first step is usually to examine the colours. Most factories used different palettes. For example, in the Meissen Kakiemon palette, the prominent colours are a greyish turquoise, sky-blue and iron-red, and the others are lemon-yellow, purple and gold. But at other factories different colours dominate, and in the original Japanese palette the turquoise is more vibrant and translucent, the yellow is dirty and there is no purple. Some factories use more gilding than others (which in this book has been referred to where relevant, as part of the palette).

The next step is to study the subject and determine whether it is Oriental or European. The subject itself can mean nothing:

many Chinese export wares were decorated with European scenes, and many of the finest European porcelains are decorated with Oriental designs. But the artists on each continent have never represented the inhabitants of the other entirely convincingly. Look at Japanese examples of the famous "Hob in the well" Kakiemon pattern (see p.38) and compare the faces with those on Meissen and Chelsea copies. It is seldom difficult to tell from these alone which continent the piece came from.

The shape and the decoration are Chinese, but this vase was made at Meissen and decorated by C. F. Herold in c.1730.

Dating

The Chinese potters were very conservative. It could take a hundred years to change a pattern. Some of their designs lasted for several centuries. As a result, it is often difficult to date Chinese wares by their decoration, but European factories were always subject to changing fashions. The style of a piece often gives a good indication of its date. In the early 18thC, designs were balanced and tightly organized.

A late Rococo Sèvres dish, c.1764.

11

HOW TO LOOK AT PORCELAIN

Even the wild Chinoiseries of J. G. Herold at Meissen were governed by a desire for symmetry. In the late 1740s, the Rococo style began to replace the Baroque. Brown and puce crept into the palettes. Designs became livelier and there was an increased use of gilding. By the mid-1750s the French royal factory at Sèvres had replaced Meissen as the leader of fashion. Under its influence, figures became more exuberant with swirling, scrolled bases, and in England they were built up with bright backdrops of applied flowers. However, it was also in France that the more disciplined Neo-classical style began to appear in the late 1750s. Shapes became rectilinear and followed the forms of classical bronzes. Bright ground colours were replaced with sepias and greys. Festoons and garlands surrounded designs in small oval and octagonal reserves.

This vase was made in Vienna c.1826, but it could just as easily have been made in Paris, Brussels, Berlin or even Worcester.

A Neo-classical Sèvres plate, c. 1785

At the end of the 18thC, the second phase of Neo-classicism, which included the French Empire style, was much more self-important and sumptuous. Gilt, dark ground colours and rich grandiose decorations covered all the porcelain. Vases and other decorative pieces were often mounted on elaborate, gilded bronze stands. But by this time there was little individuality. The styles of the leading factories had become so similar that today it is often difficult to tell them apart. During the last years of Neo-classicism, especially in England, a pretentious Neo-rococo style emerged. Then came the Gothic revival, and after the Great Exhibition of 1851 the English factories produced scores of similar pastiches of almost every earlier style.

Shapes

The shape can also reveal a great deal about a piece of porcelain. Before the European potters developed their own shapes under the influence of the prevailing fashions, they drew their inspiration from other materials and other traditions. The Rococo and Neo-classical styles had their own shapes as well as decorations, but the earlier European wares followed the shapes of silverware and pottery or else copied the Oriental forms.

A Höchst teapot, c.1755, made in the shape of silverware of the day.

Figures

The styles of the individual porcelain modellers are as unique as their signatures, and the works of the greatest artists are often easily recognizable. But there are other ways in which the maker of a model can be identified. The first step is to find out how the figure was made (provided that the base is not covered over). There are basically two methods. In the first method, known as slip-casting, the liquid clay, or slip, is poured into an absorbent mould made of earthenware or plaster of Paris.

After a few hours, the mould has absorbed the liquid and a layer of clay has built up inside it to form the figure. Slip-cast figures are light and have smooth interiors which, where not covered over, show all the shapes of the exteriors. The second method, press moulding, is a more skilful operation, in which the moulder has to press the wet clay into the mould with his fingers. Figures made in this way are much heavier. They have thumb prints and an irregular surface on the interior; and light shows through where the paste is thinnest. Most Continental figures, except those made at Meissen pre-1763 and Tournai pre-1784, are slip-cast, as are all English figures except those of Bow, Plymouth, Bristol and Worcester. Most Oriental figures before c.1800 are press-moulded. Many press-moulded pieces were made in two parts and then joined together, and it is often possible to detect the seam. The bases are also very important for identification: the style can narrow the field to a small group or even a single factory. Similarly, base decorations can be a clue. At the height of the Rococo, many Frankenthal bases were covered with moss, while their Meissen equivalents were covered with flowers.

An early Frankenthal figure with typical moulded-scroll base.

Idiosyncrasies

Many factories have individual characteristics which make their wares easy to identify. For example, a lot of Bow wares are heavily potted and do not allow the light to pass through, while other wares, such as Chelsea's, are highly translucent. Chelsea in particular has an unusual characteristic in that certain patches, known as moons, look brighter and allow much more light to pass through than the rest of the body. Other idiosyncrasies include methods of firing. For example, Chelsea dishes were fired on stilts, which left three blemishes protruding from the underside. Derby wares were fired on a tripod of pads, while Chinese Dingyao and Qingbai porcelains were fired on their mouthrims, which left them unglazed.

Condition

Some collectors prefer a piece to be restored rather than left in a damaged state, but usually restoration reduces the value. If a piece has been chipped, or if it has a broken section which has been glued back on, it will usually be worth a lot more than a piece on which there is so much over-painting that it is difficult to assess the extent of the original damage.

Marks

It is important for every collector to own a good book of marks and to examine authentic pieces in auction rooms and stores. However, it is also important to regard all marks with extreme caution. Most of them reveal very little. The vast majority of Meissen and Sèvres marks are spurious. For example, after the French Revolution a large number of white Sèvres pieces were sold off to decorators who painted them in their own workshops and marked them with interlaced Ls in order to pass them off as the real thing. Similarly, most Chinese reign marks are equally misleading: Chinese potters inscribed their wares with the marks of earlier reigns out of respect for the artistry of their predecessors; and for less honourable reasons many Japanese potters put reign marks on their products in order to pass them off as Chinese. Individual potters rarely had their own mark. Since it is seldom reliable, the mark is the last thing to look at when attempting to identify a piece of porcelain.

PORCELAIN COLOURS

The colours, or enamels, used to decorate porcelain often provide an important clue to the date or origin of a piece. Some factories used such distinctive palettes that a single dominant

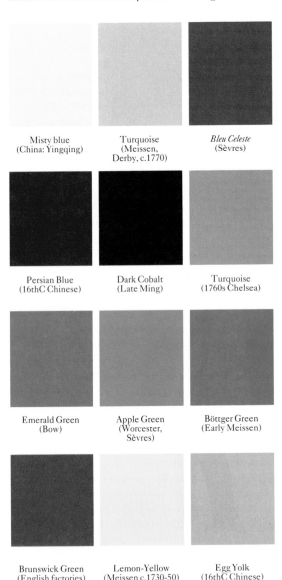

Misty blue
(China: Yingqing)

Turquoise
(Meissen,
Derby, c.1770)

Bleu Celeste
(Sèvres)

Persian Blue
(16thC Chinese)

Dark Cobalt
(Late Ming)

Turquoise
(1760s Chelsea)

Emerald Green
(Bow)

Apple Green
(Worcester,
Sèvres)

Böttger Green
(Early Meissen)

Brunswick Green
(English factories)

Lemon-Yellow
(Meissen c.1730-50)

Egg Yolk
(16thC Chinese)

colour can be enough to identify their wares. In the same way, the wrong colour can give away an otherwise convincing fake. It would be impossible to chart all the colours and tones ever used, but these two pages show the most common colours and identify the eras when they were fashionable and the manufacturers who introduced them or used them most often.

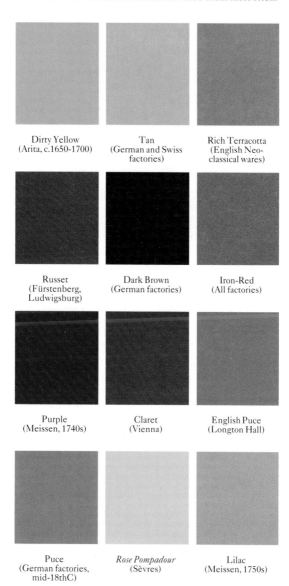

Dirty Yellow
(Arita, c.1650-1700)

Tan
(German and Swiss
factories)

Rich Terracotta
(English Neo-
classical wares)

Russet
(Fürstenberg,
Ludwigsburg)

Dark Brown
(German factories)

Iron-Red
(All factories)

Purple
(Meissen, 1740s)

Claret
(Vienna)

English Puce
(Longton Hall)

Puce
(German factories,
mid-18thC)

Rose Pompadour
(Sèvres)

Lilac
(Meissen, 1750s)

ORIENTAL PORCELAIN

A Ming wucai dish, Wanli period

Porcelain evolved slowly from the high-fired white pottery wares of northern China during the 6th and 7thC. By the beginning of the Song dynasty (960-1278) different varieties were being made all over China and also in Korea; and at the beginning of the 17thC, shortly after the Europeans had at last begun to conduct their own experiments, the Japanese probably acquired the secret from Korean prisoners who had been forcibly resettled in Kyushu.

The most famous of the early Chinese wares are the ivory-coloured Dingyao from the northern province of Hebei, which reached their peak during the 11thC. The carved patterns on these wares were also used on the celadon vessels from Yaozhou and on the pale blue or green-glazed Qingbai wares from Jingdezhen in the south, but the Dingyao versions are often more vigorous.

In about 1330, the potters of Jingdezhen began to decorate their wares under the glaze, using mostly cobalt-blue. In the following century, which is usually regarded as the classic era of coloured porcelain, the underglaze blue was used to outline a design which was then filled in after firing with several overglaze enamels. This palette, known as *doucai* (contrasting colours), was used on some of the finest of all Chinese porcelain. But the high standards of the 15thC did not long survive the arrival of Portuguese merchants in 1514. Throughout the 16thC, while the Chinese potters increased production to meet the demands of a new European market, the quality of their wares declined steadily, reaching its nadir in the repetitive patterns of mass-produced *kraak-porselein*. By the end of the century the emperor, Wanli, was so displeased with their products that he refused to allow his reign mark to be used on them.

Early in the 17thC, under the new influence of Dutch merchants, the potters of Jingdezhen began to raise their standards again. During the long, chaotic wars which marked the transition between the Ming and the Qing dynasty, they made fine, heavily potted pieces decorated with lively figures; and after about 1630 these "Transitional" wares were shipped to Holland with the lesser *kraak-porselein*.

Before the end of the 17thC almost all Chinese export porcelain was blue and white. Only wares made for the home market, known as "Imperial Wares", were decorated in the *doucai* palette or the 16thC *wucai* (five colours) palette, in which the design was painted partly in underglaze blue and partly in overglaze enamels. However, during the reign of Kangxi (1662-1722) the *wucai* palette became the basis of the famous *famille verte* decoration on export wares, and in the 18th and 19thC it was also used on the equally famous *famille rose* wares.

By the beginning of the 18thC, the Qing potters simply emulated the classic shapes and designs of earlier, more inventive generations, and in the 19thC quality declined again. Although they still made fine Imperial wares, their gaudy and over-decorated "Canton" export wares were as third-rate as the late Ming *kraak-porselein* had been.

The Japanese began to make porcelain long after the Chinese and the Koreans, but their wares are among the most admired. Sometimes bold, sometimes restrained, sometimes surprisingly ahead of their times, they are often more dynamic than their counterparts from the mainland.

According to legend, the manufacture of Japanese porcelain started in the town of Arita in 1616, after a Korean potter, Ri Sampei, found suitable clay nearby at Izumiyama. The new industry blossomed in the middle of the century, when production fell in strife-torn China and the Dutch turned to the Japanese to fulfill their orders. But when the Chinese industry recovered, Japanese wares lost their competitive edge in the European market. Although the Japanese potters raised their standards in the 1770s, they found few customers outside Japan: the Dutch merchants were preoccupied by a war in Java, and by then much of the European demand was being met by European factories, most of which were producing their own versions of Japanese Imari and Kakiemon designs. The Japanese export trade did not recover until the 1870s, when the so-called "Aesthetic Movement" revived a European interest in Japanese porcelain, but, like the Chinese equivalents, the wares were mostly second-rate and bore little resemblance to the more sophisticated wares that were being made for the home market.

MONGOLIA

NINGXIA

SHANXI

HEBEI

Ding Yao

Yaozhou Yao

SHAANZI

SICHUAN

HUBEI

C H I N A

Jingdezhen

Longqu

HUNAN

JIANGXI

FUJIAN

GUIZHOU

Dehua

GUANGDONG

GUANGXI

ORIENTAL KILN SITES

Scale

0

400

Kilometres

600

JILIN

LIAONING

Imari
Hirado
Arita
JAPAN

MING REIGN MARKS

年洪
製武
Hongwu 1368-1398

年永
製樂
Yongle 1403-1424

德大
年明宣
製
Xuande 1426-1435

化大
年明成
製
Chenghua 1465-1487

治大
年明弘
製
Hongzhi 1488-1505

德大
年明正
製
Zhengde 1506-1521

靖大
年明嘉
製
Jiajing 1522-1566

慶大
年明隆
製
Longqing 1567-1572

曆大
年明萬
製
Wanli 1573-1620

啓大
年明
製天
Tianqi 1621-1627

年崇
製禎
Chongzhen 1628-1644

QING REIGN MARKS

治大
年清順
製
Shunzhi 1644-1661

熙大
年清康
製
Kangxi 1662-1722

正大
年清雍
製
Yongzheng 1723-1735

隆大
年清乾
製
Qianlong 1736-1795

年嘉
製慶
Jiaqing 1796-1820

光大
年清道
製
Daoguang 1821-1850

豐大
年清咸
製
Xianfeng 1851-1861

治大
年清同
製
Tongzchi 1862-1874

🏯 Kiln Sites
〰〰 Province boundaries
▲▲▲ Mountain

CHINA 1: TANG AND SONG

Yingqing ewer and cover from the southern Song dynasty
c.1127-1279; ht 6 ¹⁄₂in/16.5cm; value code D

Identification checklist for Tang porcelain
1. Is the paste greyish and granular?
2. Is the glaze creamy?
3. Does the glaze stop in an irregular line above the foot?
4. Can the weals caused by the potter's knife be seen and felt?
5. Has the glaze gathered in dark pools?
6. Is the piece small, less than approx 8in/20cm?

Identification checklist for Dingyao porcelain
7. Is the glaze warm and ivory coloured?
8. Has it gathered in brown or olive pools?
9. Is the piece unglazed around the mouth rim, or is the rim bound in copper?
10. Is the decoration carved or moulded?
11. Is the decoration surrounded by a squared scroll?

Identification checklist for Yingqing porcelain
12. Are the shapes and decorations similar to Dingyao?
13. Is the glaze bluish?
14. Have any unglazed areas burned red in the firing (e.g. on the mouthrim)?

Tang porcelain (618-906)
Porcelain was first produced in the north of China during the Tang dynasty and almost certainly evolved from the white-bodied wares produced during the preceding Sui dynasty.

The early porcelain is greyish white and granular, not unlike wet chalk. The glaze has a creamy appearance and is often quite casually applied, leaving a wavy line where it falls short of the base. It also has a tendency to dribble down the sides of the piece and gather in dark pools.

Tang porcelain is seldom more than 8in/20cm high and follows the shapes of the simplest contemporary pottery and metalwork. All hollow wares, such as this bowl, have bulbous sides and small, slightly splayed feet.
* Beneath the thin glaze, the concentric weals caused by the potter's knife can be clearly seen and felt.
* The footrim has an irregular thickness, and the interior wall slopes inwards towards the base.
* Some dishes have plain rims, others have notches, and some, like the example *above*, have neat lobes, suggesting a rudimentary flower-head.
* The northern Song porcelain had a strong influence on Korean ceramics, particularly on celadon wares. It was made for the Prince of Yueh, after whom it was named.

Dingyao porcelain is decorated either with carving or moulding. The most common themes are fruit, birds or, as on the dish pictured *above left*, flowers and leaves.
* The decorations are often enclosed within one or two bands of squared scroll, a design that is very similar to the Greek key motif.
* As the pieces were fired upside-down, the plain rims were protected against chipping by the application of copper rims or bands. Most of these copper rims have not survived.
* The double-gourd ewer on the *right* epitomizes early Song porcelain. The rhythmic outlines, the sinuous handle and the curving spout are all typical.
* These shapes were prototypes for generations of Chinese wares.

Southern Song (1127-1279)

The wares produced at the southern kilns in Jiangxi continued the traditions of the northern Song dynasty, with very little change in the basic shapes. The notches and flares on the rims of bowls are a little less pronounced, and the footrims tend to be very thin and short, but the much more obvious difference lies in the composition of the paste and the glaze.

Despite the wealth and splendour of the age, most Tang porcelain is undecorated, but this rare mortar, based on a bronze form, has sides that have been individually carved with lions' masks.

Northern Song (960-1127)

During the northern Song dynasty porcelain became more refined and the potters paid greater attention to detail. The famous porcelain of this period comes from Hebei and Henan and is known as Dingyao. It is covered in a warm, ivory glaze, which is finished in a neat line around the foot and has a strong brown or olive tone where it has pooled.

Yingqing Porcelain

The porcelain of Jiangxi, known as Yingqing, is whiter than Dingyao, although the high iron content, which oxidizes in the firing, causes it to burn red in places where it has not been glazed.
* The translucent glaze has a pale watery blue or even green colour. These colours vary in intensity, as can be seen on the ewer in the main picture.
* The glaze, which gave the southern Song porcelain its name (Yingqing means "misty blue"), also has the effect of making the wares look cooler than those produced in the northern province.

CHINA 2: YUAN

A Longquan celadon vase
Yuan Dynasty (1279-1368); ht 27in/68.5cm; value code C/D

Identification checklist for Yuan porcelain
1. Is the glaze bluish or greenish?
2. Is the glaze thick and suffused with bubbles (Longquan)?
3. Has the footrim been cut crudely with a knife?
4. Have the unglazed areas fired red?
5. Is there a great deal of carved or applied decoration?
6. If the piece is a vase, is the lower portion carved with very long stiff leaves (Longquan)?
7. If the piece is blue and white, are there places where the blue is pale greyish or very dark?
8. If the piece is blue and white, are there patches of black oxidization on the cobalt?
9. Is the painted decoration very crowded?
10. Do plates and dishes have barbed rims?
11. If the piece is a figure, is it Yingqing (see p.23)?

The Yuan Dynasty, 1279-1368

The Yuan emperors were the Mongol descendants of Genghis Khan. Until recently, it was thought that their reign was a period of little merit as far as ceramics were concerned, but it is now recognized as a time of considerable importance. The potters who continued to produce the traditional stonewares and porcelains were just as accomplished as their predecessors under the Song, and it was in the middle years of the Yuan dynasty that they perfected the technique of decorating porcelains in underglaze colours.

Longquan

In terms of body and glaze, Yuan porcelains differ only slightly from the porcelains of the previous dynasties, but they are very different in size and in the complexity of their decoration. Many of them, particularly the heavily potted wares from Longquan, are much larger, and they can be crowded with as many as nine different decorative bands. As on the vase in the main picture, the lower parts of large vessels are often carved with very long stiff leaves. * As dishes were fired on a circular collar, they have wide unglazed rings inside their bases, and in common with hollow wares they have footrims which have been cut off crudely with the potters' knives. Longquan wares have a white body (except in the unglazed places where it has burned red) and their glaze is thick and suffused with bubbles.

During the Yuan dynasty the Chinese potters used cobalt-blue to develop the style of decoration that was to become known as blue and white. Cobalt-blue is one of the few ceramic colours which can withstand the high temperature necessary to fuse the porcelain glaze. By painting it directly onto the porcelain and then covering it with the glaze, the potters were able to create complex decorations which could survive the firing and last as long as the porcelain itself. This vase is typical of the Yuan blue and white wares – there are eight different bands of complex decorations – and if the lid had survived it would have made the ninth. The underglaze cobalt is pale greyish in some areas and very dark in others.

In common with other wares of this period, the footrim on this dish has been cut with a knife, the unglazed area has fired red, and the glaze itself is irregular and has a distinct bluish tinge.

Yingqing wares continued under the Yuan emperors, but they lost their subtle simplicity. Many of them were overwhelmed by cut-through panels and applied beadwork and strands. Even on this stem cup, which is comparatively restrained, the decoration interrupts the natural lines of the vessel, and the handles are much too dominant.

Figures from the period are relatively rare, but some Yingqing figures were made for export to the Philippines. Most are less than 5in (12.7cm) tall: at 11in (28cm), this example is exceptional.

23

A Ming blue and white ewer
Yongle (1403-25) ht 11 ⁷/₈ in/30.2cm: value code A

Identification checklist for Imperial Ming porcelain

1. Is the glaze thick, bubbled and greenish or bluish (early 15thC)?
2. Is the glaze thin, smoky or yellowish (Chenghua)?
3. Have the unglazed areas fired red?
4. Is there any "heaping and piling" (see *below*)?
5. Has the footrim been trimmed with a knife?
6. Is the foot undercut (see *opposite*)?
7. Is the foot tall in proportion to the rest of the vessel?
8. Is it possible to detect the seam where the two parts of a hollow vessel have been joined together?
9. If the piece is polychrome, is the design outlined in underglaze blue, or is an underglaze blue wash part of the palette?
10. Is there a reign mark?

The Ming Dynasty, 1369-1644

The last 30 years of the 14thC saw a transition between the robust and complex wares of the Yuan and the brilliant and balanced wares of the Ming. Under the Ming emperors, the potters of Jingdezhen refined their materials and techniques and organized their designs so as to complement the shapes of their dishes and vessels, as in the ewer in the main picture, rather than overwhelm them.

* On most Ming pieces there are still a few patches where concentrations of cobalt have broken through the glaze in firing and oxidized black, creating an effect which became known in Europe as "heaping and piling". During the 18thC, when techniques had improved sufficiently to eliminate the fault, the Qing potters tried to reproduce it by overloading their brushes, but the results always look contrived.

Contrary to popular belief, not all Ming wares are decorated in underglaze blue, as this Ming bottle testifies. At the end of the 14thC, during the reign of Hongwu, the Chinese were forbidden to travel abroad. As a result they were unable to obtain cobalt from Persia and instead they used copper, producing a rare underglaze which ranges from pinkish red to silver-grey.
* Like all Ming wares, this bottle has an undercut foot (that is, it slopes inwards).
* All Ming hollow vessels were made in two parts, and it is usually possible to detect the seam where the top and bottom are joined.

Reign marks
The reign mark of Yongle consists of four characters. For subsequent reigns the marks usually comprise a double circle containing two columns with three characters in each.

The first polychrome wares, such as this delicate little "chicken cup", *below*, which is only 3in/7.6cm in diameter, were produced during the reign of

Chenghua (1465-87). In a palette known as *doucai*, the design was first outlined in underglaze blue and then painted after firing in:-
* iron-red
* yellow
* green
* manganese-brown
* black.
* As the potters had by this time changed to a thinner, smoky or yellowish glaze, the blue beneath it is much sharper than it had been previously.

The slightly blurred effect on the design of this wine cup made in the reign of Yongle (1403-25), is typical of the early 15thC, when the thick bubbled glaze was still being used.
* As on most Ming pieces, the foot is comparatively tall in relation to the rest of the vessel.
* Scrolled flowers are the most common of all Chinese designs.
* The piece bears the mark of the Emperor Yongle – the earliest known reign mark on underglaze-decorated porcelain.

This pen box, made in the second half of the 16thC, is painted boldly in the *wucai* palette, in which the underglaze blue is painted as a wash and forms only part of the design.
* The colours are the same as in the *doucai* palette, but the tones are different. For example, the underglaze blue has a strong purple tinge.
* The casual brushwork on this piece is typical of the later Ming period, when the standard of painting declined.

CHINA 4: IMPERIAL QING

A Qing bowl
Kangxi (1662-1722); ht 5in/12.7cm; value code C/D

Identification checklist for Imperial Qing porcelain, 1644-1912
1. Has the paste fired creamy white in unglazed areas?
2. Has the piece been covered with a coloured glaze?
3. Is it decorated in the *famille verte* or *famille rose* palette? (see *opposite*)
4. Is the decoration a precise and mechanical copy of Song and Ming patterns? (see pp. 20-1 and 24-5)
5. Are there no visible joins on hollow wares?
6. Is the piece very neatly finished?
7. Is the base of the piece flat?
8. Is there a script or seal character reign mark?

The Qing Dynasty, 1644-1912

During the long wars which marked the end of the Ming dynasty and the beginning of the Qing, the production for the home market at Jingdezhen declined dramatically. In 1675 the kilns were destroyed in a fire, and for several years production ceased altogether. But in 1682 the second Qing emperor, Kangxi, appointed a new supervisor for the imperial kilns and during the rest of his reign, which lasted until 1722, the Chinese potters produced some of their finest porcelain.

Kangxi wares

The Qing potters continued the traditional styles and in particular made painstakingly accurate copies of the classical wares of the Song and early Ming periods. But the long reign of Kangxi was also a great period of innovation:-
* A new paste and new glazes were developed.
* New palettes were introduced.
* Glazing became more even and potting more accurate and economical. Pieces were much more neatly finished – there are no knife marks on the bases of Qing wares, and no visible joins on pots and vases.

Paste and glaze

The paste used during the Qing dynasty contains a larger proportion of kaolin and less iron than the paste used under the Ming emperors. It is therefore much whiter, and there is no iron oxidization in unglazed areas.
* The Qing potters introduced or rediscovered a large number of coloured glazes, many of which were derived from copper.

This beautiful beehive-shaped water pot, made towards the end of the reign of Kangxi, is covered in "peach bloom", the rarest of the copper-based glazes.
* The original Ming version of this glaze was a dull liver colour, but the Qing potters transformed it into a pinkish red suffused with pale mushroom patches and mossy green flecks.

This early 18thC saucer dish has been decorated in the *famille verte* palette with typical delicacy and attention to detail. One of the first new palettes to appear during the reign of the emperor Kangxi, *famille verte* is basically an evolution of the *wucai* palette in which the dominant colour is a brilliant green. Although the colours are slightly lighter in tone, the only real difference is that underglaze blue has been replaced by overglaze blue.

In the early 18thC, a new enamel was introduced into China from

Europe, which could be used to produce most shades of pink. This became the basis of an almost pastel-shaded palette, *famille rose*, in which white was added to make the other colours opaque. This pair of vases, made during the reign of Qianlong (1736-95), is superbly painted with blossoming branches and rockwork, one of the favourite themes on early *famille rose* wares.

This dragon bowl and its dome cover have been decorated in the Qing revival of the Ming *doucai* palette. The colours are reproduced exactly. The only real difference is that in this version the painting is more mechanical and precise. On the unglazed strip around the footrim, where the Ming wares fired red, the new paste has fired creamy white. The reign mark of the emperor Yongzheng (1723-35) can be seen on the base.

Even if it was not possible to see the reign mark of the emperor Qianlong (1736-95), it would still be easy to identify this Ming-style vase as a Qing copy:-
* The design is extremely precise.
* The cobalt has been dressed to look as though it is heaped and piled (see p. 24), but the patches have been made to fit the pattern. The whole effect is much too contrived to be convincing.

CHINA 5: MING EXPORT

A late Ming blue and white jar
c.1640; ht 16in/40cm; value code C/D

Identification checklist for Ming export porcelain, 1369-1644
1. Are the paste and the glaze typical of Ming wares (see p. 24)?
2. Does the piece combine a European shape with Chinese decoration? (post-1600)
3. Is the design broken up into numerous panels?
4. If the piece is in the *wucai* palette, is it casually painted?
5. Is the base carelessly finished?
6. Is there a reign mark (see p.25)?

Ming Export Porcelain

The Chinese have been exporting porcelain since at least the 9thC. During the Song and Yuan dynasties, they were distributing their wares throughout Southeast Asia, India and the Middle East, but it was only with the arrival of the Portuguese navigators in 1514 that they began to export in large quantities to Europe. From about 1520 onwards, Portuguese carracks were carrying thousands of pieces of porcelain into Lisbon every year, and eventually the Dutch, the French, the English, the Swedes and the Danes were following their example. The extra demand on the potters of Jingdezhen resulted in mass production and the employment of unskilled labour, and inevitably standards declined.

Shapes and types of ware

Until almost the end of the reign of the Emperor Wanli (1573-1619) the shapes of export wares reflected either the Chinese taste or else that of old-established customers in Asia and the Middle East. The most common objects are:-
* dishes
* bowls
* vases
* ewers
* kendis (Hindu ritual vessels).
However, at the beginning of the 17thC the potters widened their range to appeal to the European taste and began to make copies of Western silverware, such as:-
* salts
* spouted jugs
* tankards
* candlesticks.

Designs

Most of the early Ming export wares were decorated in underglaze blue in the traditional Chinese designs, but those made after the beginning of the 17thC can be divided into two distinct groups, known as *kraak-porselein* and "Transitional" wares.

Kraak-porselein

On *kraak-porselein*, which is often quite casually painted, the design is broken up into panels enclosing repeating motifs of flowers, animals or birds. The usual form is a dish on which alternating wide and narrow panels radiate from a central hexagon.

The pierced border was introduced on export wares towards the end of the reign of Wanli. This example, which has been sketchily painted, was probably made for Japan.

"Transitional" wares

The word "Transitional" describes the period between the death of Wanli in 1619 and the accession of the first Qing emperor in 1662, when the last Ming princes were struggling unsuccessfully to repel the Manchu. In the absence of imperial patronage, Jingdezhen painters decorated export wares with traditional animals, flowers and figures.

Most Chinese kendis, Hindu ritual vessels, were exported to the Middle East, where they became bases for hookahs. This stylized elephant-shaped example has a saddle cloth decorated with a complex diaper typical of late Ming export ware.
* The horizontal seam or bulge where the two parts were joined is just visible below the tassels.

This dish, sketchily painted in the *wucai* palette around 1630, was also made for the Japanese market. In general, two types of wares were exported to Japan. The first, known as *shonzui*, is decorated with complex but meticulously painted brocade patterns and repeating diapers. The second, *ko-sometsuke*, is casually painted with barren landscapes and animals or wandering ascetics. This rare example combines both.

This candlestick, made in the reign of Wanli, combines a European metalwork shape with traditional Chinese designs.

Although the vast majority of Ming wares exported to Europe were blue and white, a few were in the *wucai* palette. This "Transitional" vase, made around 1650, is decorated in typical broad washes of blue, emerald-green and iron-red.
* The footrim has fired red.

29

CHINA 6: QING EXPORT

*A Qianlong armorial dish
1736-95; ht 12½in/31.75cm; value code B/C*

Identification checklist for Kangxi, 1662-1722
1. Is the glaze thin and glassy?
2. On blue and white wares, is the blue cold and steely?
3. If polychrome, is it decorated in an Imari or *famille verte* palette?
Identification checklist for Yongzheng and Qianlong, 1723-95
4. Is the glaze thick, bluish and rippled?
5. Is there sugary-like accretion on the base?
6. Is the piece painted in opaque *famille rose* enamels?
7. If a figure, is it press-moulded? (1662-1795)
8. Has it a European form? (1662-1795)

Qing Export
When the imperial kilns had been rebuilt, the Chinese set out to recover their export trade, and this time, in addition to the blue and white, they made polychrome wares in order to satisfy the European taste created by Imari and Kakiemon.

Armorial services
During the 17thC the Dutch and then the English became the largest European buyers, which is why there are so many *famille verte* wares in England today. A significant proportion of this trade consisted of private orders for dinner services decorated with the customers' coats of arms.

These three vases were made c.1700, when mass production techniques had reached their peak. The designs, which by then were much more complicated, were broken up into petal-shaped zones, and each zone was then decorated by a different painter.

* The blue is now very cool and steely, rather than purplish, and from 1700 onwards the sharpness of the decoration is emphasized by the thinness of the glaze.
* The vases and other vessels of this period are also more thinly potted and lighter-looking than earlier vessels.

This *famille rose* dish depicting *The Doctor's Visit* was designed by a Dutchman, Cornelis Pronk. In the 1730s, Pronk was commissioned by the Dutch East India Company to design a series of Oriental plates for the European market. The result is an awkward Chinese copy of a European version of a Chinese concept, but it was through orders such as this that the Chinese painters acquired the more developed European sense of perspective.

After blue and white, the most common export palette was *famille verte*. This large dish, which is 2ft/61cm across, has a central panel depicting the most popular 18thC theme – a fenced rock garden – and petal-shaped reserves containing almost the entire repertoire of designs for export wares: flowers, landscapes, the hundred antiques (which were the various shapes of vases), the eight precious objects and the eight Buddhist emblems. Only figures are missing.
* As usual, the panels are set on a green or red ground covered with scrolling foliage.

After the Declaration of Independence, the United States began trading directly with China, rather than through England, and soon afterwards pieces were made to fulfil private orders. This tureen, made in the most popular European shape at the beginning of the 19thC, depicts the surrender of General Burgoyne at Saratoga.

At the beginning of the 18thC, the Chinese potters began to copy more complicated European shapes. This ewer and basin, made around 1730, owe nothing in design and form to Chinese culture. Their shape is pure European Rococo, and they are painted in the Japanese Imari palette.

The technique of painting almost entirely in black and grey, *en grisaille*, was introduced to China by the Jesuits soon after 1727, and was often used for architectural scenes, such as the European factories on the waterfront at Canton, on this European-shaped punch bowl.

31

KOREA

A high-shouldered dragon jar,
17thC; ht 16in/40.6cm; value code B/C

Identification checklist for Korean porcelain
1. Has the porcelain oxidized on unglazed areas?
2. Is the porcelain greenish or bluish?
3. Is there a brown stained crackle in the glaze?
4. Is the footrim crudely pared with a knife?
5. Is there any large-grained kiln grit on the foot?
6. Has the body split in the firing, or if large, has it warped or sagged?
7. Is the underglaze decoration vigorous?
8. Does the piece look hand-made?
9. Is the main body of the piece faceted, while the remainder is not (see *opposite*)?

Korean porcelain

The manufacture of porcelain in Korea probably began in the 11th or 12thC. Initially influenced by contemporary porcelain in China, especially Qingbai, the earliest wares were left in the white and relied for their appeal entirely on their moulded shapes, which were derived from either flowers or other vegetation.

Underglaze decorations were introduced in the 15thC, probably after similar wares had been received as gifts from the Chinese.

As in China, the difficulty of obtaining sufficient supplies of cobalt for the blue meant that copper-red and iron-grey were sometimes used as substitutes. The range of shapes and types of decoration on Korean porcelain are the most idiosyncratic of all Oriental ceramics, which makes them among the easiest to identify. Always animated, they are imbued with the individual personalities of the potters and painters who made them.
* Korean porcelain is unmarked.

Paste and glaze

Korean paste is off-white and has to be heavily potted because of ts over-plasticity. The clay tends to split, probably because of its heavy construction, and the larger pieces often sag in the firing. Since it seems to be more absorbent than other Asian porcelains, the material tends to discolour, and on pre-17thC wares the exposed body often burns brown, due to the presence of iron in its composition.
* The glaze usually looks bluish or greenish. On some pieces there are areas of irregular crackle; and the glaze has a tendency to lift off or flake.

Decoration

The most common subject for decoration is the dragon. Another very common design consists of small circular reserves placed at random around the vessel, enclosing grasses or simplified vegetation.
* Other designs include the tiger, the tortoise, the crane, and other animals.
* It was not until the 18thC that the Korean painters began to decorate their wares with figure subjects.

This ovoid form with almost straight sides and a thickly painted design are typical of early Korean decorated wares.
* The scaly fish among rocks are applied in the finger painting style, in which very thick lines are drawn very quickly with a finger.
* Most of these vases have a short straight neck and a similarly shaped foot.
* This example has a fine network of crackle on one side only.

The most sophisticated Korean products were the pierced and carved wares, such as this brush pot – a very fashionable item in the 18th and 19thC.

This blue and white baluster vase, vigorously painted with a four-clawed Korean dragon, has many of the typical characteristics of Korean porcelain:
* the shape is one of the most common on Korean wares throughout the 17thC
* the porcelain has burned to a shiny, rusty red on the exposed edge of the foot where the glaze has fallen short
* the footrim is spattered with specks of kiln grit
* there is a ridge just above the foot, and the neck is straight, wide and relatively tall
* the cloud formation looks almost like a peony.

The Korean potters were particularly fond of making vessels of which the main body was angular and faceted. This eleven-sided jar was made in the 16th or 17thC, when cobalt was difficult to obtain, and it has been decorated in an exceptionally fine tone of underglaze copper red. The design consists of random circular reserves containing reeds.
* The interrupted series of petal-panels on the neck is quite unlike any other Oriental border.
* There are pinholes in the body of the glaze, kiln grit has adhered to the foot, and the unglazed area on the footrim has oxidized in the firing.

JAPAN 1: BLUE AND WHITE

*A large Arita dish made for export
late 17thC; ht 15¾in/40cm; value code C*

Identification checklist for Japanese porcelain
1. Is the porcelain more granular than Chinese porcelain?
2. Are there traces of iron-red in the exposed body?
3. Is the piece heavily potted?
4. If a vessel, has it sagged slightly in the kiln?
5. If a dish, are there three or more spur marks on the underside?
6. Is the underglaze blue extremely dark (Imari), or soft (Nabeshima), or does it range from washed out to almost black? (Blue and white)
7. Does the piece have a geometric profile? (Kakiemon)
8. Is the rim dressed in iron-brown glaze? (Kakiemon and Arita)

Arita wares
The earliest recorded Japanese porcelain was made in the Arita district of northern Kyusha Island from c.1610. Japanese potters learnt the techniques from craftsmen who settled there in the late 16thC after Hideyoshi brought them back from his expedition to Korea. Blue and white was one of many kinds of porcelain made at the Arita kilns for the export trade as well as the domestic market. During the

second quarter of the 17thC, the Arita porcelain industry grew rapidly until there were about 30 kilns operating in the area.
* As well as blue and white, Imari, Kakiemon, Polychrome, Nabeshima, Hirado, Fukagawa and Makuzu wares (see pp. 36-41) were all produced at kilns in and around Arita.

Japanese blue and white
Like the Chinese blue and white wares, the Japanese versions were

decorated with an underglaze blue cobalt oxide before being glazed and fired. The resulting tones varied enormously according to the impurities in the ore and how much colour had been applied. They ranged from greyish or blackish blue to sapphire. Occasionally, the potters would add blue after glazing to hide the blurring that sometimes occurred during firing.

Wares made for the Japanese domestic market

Japanese blue and white porcelain was divided into two main types, one for the domestic market and one for export. The pieces made for home use were generally small-scale dishes and hollow wares. Many of them were casually painted with spare landscapes and vegetation copied from Korean designs. But during the 17thC, the Arita potters also began producing more refined pieces to satisfy the demands of Japanese tea drinkers.

Export wares

When the civil wars of the mid-17thC almost halted the production of Chinese porcelain, Dutch merchants persuaded the Japanese potters to fill the gap in the market by making wares specially for the European taste. The plate in the main picture, which is marked with the cipher of the Dutch East India Company, is typical but is more blurred than a Chinese original.

The *enghalskrug* (or narrow necked jug), illustrated here is a European shape, decorated in the traditional Chinese style.

The pear-shaped *birnkrug, above, right*, is a drinking vessel, also made to European specification. The border decoration is very

characteristic of 17th and early 18thC Japanese porcelain. It derives from Chinese Tang dynasty vine scrolls, and is termed *karakusa* or octopus scrollwork. Other common ancillary motifs include chrysanthemum petal collars, interlaced "cash" symbols and short leaves. Arita porcelain of this type is difficult to chip.

Other Chinese-style features

Many other Chinese features appear, in addition to those shown here. These include:
* Segmental or panelled designs surrounding a central pictorial element which copied Chinese *kraak-porselein*. This style was called *fuyo-de* in Japan and was mainly used on open shapes such as bowls and dishes.
* Coarse pastiches of Chinese Transitional wares from the late Ming/early Qing period, depicting more open patterns, often of semi-botanical subjects and narrative themes. This decoration was usually found on closed shapes, such as jars, bottles and vases.
* Loose brushwork owing to the fact that Japanese potters had to work from sketchily decorated wooden models of Chinese originals supplied by the Dutch.
* A thick, greyish bubble glaze that tends to blur the image.
* A "musliny" surface which resembles 15thC Chinese blue and white wares.

As well as drawing inspiration from China, many pieces were also based on the shapes of European stoneware, pottery, metal and even glass.

Firing

When dishes and bowls were being fired in the kiln, they were supported on three or more spurs or stilts of porcelain to prevent them from sagging. The spurs were attached to the piece within the footrim on the base and stood on the floor or the saggar. These never occur on Chinese wares.

JAPAN 2: IMARI AND POLYCHROME

Imari

This type of porcelain was one of the largest groups made for the Western market. Like the blue and white and Kakiemon wares, it came from the Arita district. The name originates from the port of Imari through which most of the export porcelain was shipped. However, the Europeans used the name to distinguish enamelled wares from blue and white.

Like the covered bowl *above*, Imari pieces were generally first painted in underglaze blue, then glazed and fired, then enamelled in colours which included iron-red, and gilded and fired once more.

Enamels

Although the most typical Imari palette consisted of dark underglaze blue, red and gold, there were variations according to date, type and price range:
* Prominent in the early Imari palette is a strong aubergine.
* Among the earliest polychrome wares are those decorated in underglaze blue, iron-red and gold and silver, recorded as being shipped to China in the 1640s.
* In many of the best-quality Imari wares where there is no underglaze blue, decoration is usually a rich polychrome or else a more restricted palette.
* For their least expensive products, Imari enamellers often used a palette of red and gilding with an outline of black over a dark, purplish-blue underglaze.
* In the best pieces with underglaze blue, the potters used a much wider palette, of red, blue, yellow, two greens, aubergine and black.

Underglaze blue

The blue underglaze played a variety of roles:
* In early pieces (late 17th/early 18thC), it was applied as circumferential lines or patterns to divide the piece into zones which could be filled with enamel colours. The enamelled areas were often confined to the middle of a bowl or vessel, or to the well of a dish.
* In later pieces, the enamellers usually had to follow specific guidelines laid down in the blue underglaze by the painters. Here, the colour was used to define areas of decoration and for the basis of the pictorial design itself.
* In contrasting areas of design, notably with fan-shaped or scroll-shaped reserves against a powder-blue ground.
* In other pieces, the underglaze blue is like a patterned or floral shadow seen behind or beside the more definite colours and images.

Types of Imari wares

Imari wares were usually large display pieces designed to complement the grand interiors of European houses. Apart from tablewares and room ornaments such as vases and bottles, figures were also exported, as they exemplified Japan's exoticism to the West. These could either be freestanding, or used as decorative knobs for lids.

In the 18th and 19thC, Imari potters produced sets of three jars and two trumpet-shaped vases which were intended to ornament fireplaces during the summer months. The set shown *above* dates from 1700-20 and exhibits the growing fashion for jars with prominent lids and knobs. In some examples, these features were so big that they seem out of proportion to the rest of the piece. Such groups were called *garnitures de cheminée*.

Decorative themes

Imari wares were decorated in rich brocade patterns, like that of the covered bowl on the previous page. The panels usually contained figures, flowers or animals superimposed over backgrounds depicting flowers or flowers and blossoming branches. In the Imari wares with underglaze blue, landscape and floral decoration predominate. Some pieces were also ornamented in high relief, and occasionally had figural knobs. In the 19thC, the style began to lose its former vitality. Shapes became top-heavy and decoration less vigorous.

Polychrome wares

The Japanese potters also produced a range of polychrome wares which, like the mainstream Imari pieces, were intended only for export to the West. They are less common than the other export wares, and most of them have European shapes.

In general, the style of decoration on these polychrome export wares is lighter than it is in the dense Imari patterns, and often bears a closer resemblance to the Kakiemon style.

This polychrome box and cover were made in the late 17thC and show the blurred underglaze blue typical of Arita porcelain in general. The thick knobbly scrollwork is called *karakusa* (see also pp. 34-5) and is also characteristic of Japanese wares from this period.

This vase is a late 19thC example of Imari ware, showing how the style gradually lost its vitality. The decoration seems fussy and the colours are not nearly so intense as in 17th and 18thC pieces. The Indian club shape was very popular for vases at this time.

Copies

In the early 18thC, Chinese potters began making reproductions of the mundane blue, red and gold Imari pieces which were then known as Chinese Imari. The Chinese also made copies of the more expensive polychrome wares.

In Europe, imitation Imari was manufactured at Delft in Holland, at Ansbach in Germany, by the Vezzi factory in Venice, and, in the 19thC, by several English firms as well.

The bottle *above*, made c.1660-70, is based on a Dutch model with double rings around the mouth. It was one of the earliest European shapes to appear in Arita porcelain, and was probably similar to the bottle ordered in thousands for the Dutch East India Company's Batavian apothecary's shop. The decoration is loosely based on late Ming Chinese wares, but the combination of red, green and yellow is distinctively Japanese.

JAPAN 3: KAKIEMON

A Kakiemon vase

Kakiemon

Kakiemon wares derive their name from the semi-legendary figure of Sakaida Kakiemon, who is said to have invented the enamelling process in Japan. They represent a more restricted range than Imari wares generally, being confined to small dishes, bowls, bottles and vases. Kakiemon wares belong to the more sophisticated end of the market.

The porcelain emerged as a coherent group by the 1680s, some years after the Kakiemon kilns were set up. The distinctive features are:
* a unique, milky-white body, called *nigoshide*, covered with an almost colourless glaze. The term Kakiemon is associated with porcelain sparingly painted in over-glaze enamels, and also with kilns which produced blue and white porcelain
* a geometric profile: one tradition has it that Japanese potters could

not throw circular pieces
* a special palette consisting of brilliant enamels in iron-red, sky blue, turquoise, pale manganese, dirty yellow and black, as shown in the bottle on the previous page.
* the painting on all Kakiemon wares, which is of high quality
* open shapes such as bowls and dishes. Closed shapes were found at the site, but they, too, must have been brought in ready-made from other kilns
* the pieces were often dressed with iron brown edges which were meant to prevent chipping. However, many extant examples are damaged.

Perhaps the most famous pattern, copied at Meissen, Chelsea and Bow, was the "Hob in the well" design, the title inspired by an early 18thC play.

Note
Most Kakiemon pieces seem to have been made at one kiln, but similar wares were also made by rival kilns, and at the present time it is not always possible to tell which site they came from.

Identification
Less gorgeous than Imari wares and not so bold as Arita blue and white, most export enamelled Kakiemon has a distinctive palette of reds and blues, a usually dead white body and delicate, freely flowing patterns and is more refined than Imari or other Arita wares.

This decagonal dish dating from the late 17thC exhibits many typical Kakiemon features. Here the reds and blues predominate over the other colours, and the design is both spare and asymmetrical. The prowling tiger motif was very popular.

The piece illustrated *above* is in biscuit porcelain and was modelled on a European stoneware tankard. The carved and moulded shallow relief on the sides is very unusual. It must have been imported into the Kakiemon kiln for decoration. The decorators used a popular theme representing calm water that was derived from textile decoration and was often seen on Samurai kimonos.
* The reddish brown colour is achieved by leaving the body unglazed and allowing the iron to oxidize in the firing.

Imitations

There were many imitations of Kakiemon porcelain and sherds of *nigoshide* have been found at two other kilns in Arita. The style of painting was frequently copied and the enamels were often used in other decorative styles. Some imitations include additional enamel colours, such as brown, which was used in "Hampton Court" hexagonal jars.

Although the Kakiemon style was rarely imitated in China, it provided an enormous stimulus to the French, German and English porcelain industries. The shape of the bottle illustrated on p. 37 was copied by Meissen (see p.49) and also in England by Chelsea (see p.113).

Meissen wares are more glassy in appearance, and their palette is very different. Their yellows are much clearer and their turquoise is more like a milky greyish blue. Chelsea pieces are warmer and creamier, and they were made of soft-paste porcelain, which allowed the colours to sink into the glaze. Kakiemon ware was also imitated by European earthenware manufacturers and the more sophisticated porcelain factories.

The figure of a boy on a drum shown *above* was made in c.1680. Figural or animal statuettes were rare in Kakiemon wares; the most common subjects were actors or geisha. Arita kilns produced several figures of boys, many of which had the same head. However, this piece has the Kakiemon palette which makes it especially valuable.

The Meissen and Chelsea factories reproduced the decoration as well as the form of this late 17thC flared-rim Kakiemon tea or wine cup, one of a pair. At 4in/10cm high, it is taller than average for Kakiemon wares, and from above shows a typical octagonal section. Other authentic characteristics include:
* a palette dominated by iron-red and blue
* the alternating pine and *prunus* blossom decorations on the sides
* the isolated *mon*, or flower heads.

JAPAN 4: NABESHIMA & HIRADO

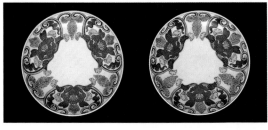

These Nabeshima plates have typical stylized decoration (see below.)

Nabeshima wares

The most refined of all Japanese porcelain was made in Arita exclusively for the Nabeshima clan, who governed the region. According to legend, a new factory was established in 1660 to make wares for the feudal lords or for presentation to the Shogun. It was forbidden to sell any but the rejects and as a result few specimens of Nabeshima ware are known in the West.

Characteristic features of Nabeshima porcelain are:
* an off-white and virtually flawless body covered in a greyish or bluish glaze
* tall footrims on shallow wares, such as saucer dishes
* thin and very even potting, resulting in a shape that is a pure parabola with little variation in thickness.

Palette

Underglaze blue wares and celadon glaze wares are very rare in Nabeshima. Most pieces were first painted with an underglaze blue outline and then coloured with the following range of enamels, which were similar to the Ming *doucai* palette:
* iron-red
* green
* yellow
* manganese
* black.

Decoration

The most common decorative themes in Nabeshima ware are:
* stylized leaves and flowers, as on the two plates *above*
* repeating geometric patterns such as *seigaha* (calm water), trellis or cash (see *right*)
* simple, realistic studies of birds, flowers, fruit and aquatic themes.

The most characteristic features of Nabeshima wares are found on the undersides of the dishes which are decorated with a series of interlocking coins with ribbons. These are known as "cash" symbols (Oriental coins were pierced so that they could be carried on a cord). The exterior of the tall foot, which is more than half an inch (1.27cm) in height, is invariably decorated with a comb pattern known as *Kusitakade*, which was a speciality of Nabeshima wares.

Hirado

In the late 18th and early 19thC the Hirado kilns produced fine blue and white porcelain almost equal in quality to Nabeshima wares. Among the factory's most popular products are white figures of children and animals, sometimes decorated here and there with a subtle blue colouring. The pure white clay allowed for modelling of the highest order. The details and the folds of the clothes are almost as sharp as the carving on a *netsuke*.

The most typical, and also the most admired, of the Hirado products are the blue and white wares, such as this late 19thC vase. It has a soft greyish blue underglaze.

The decorative themes were either figure subjects, especially children playing, or misty pine-clad landscapes, and these were often set between borders of cash symbols, geometric patterns or stiff, stylized leaves.

Perhaps the most accomplished of all the 20thC porcelain manufacturers in Japan is Makuzu Kozan, whose great technical mastery of underglaze colours, such as yellow, pink, green and of course cobalt, can be seen clearly on this piece. Occasionally, Kozan bases his designs, which were almost always natural subjects, on a celebrated painting and signs it in underglaze blue.

One of the most important modern porcelain factories in Japan is the Fukagawa Porcelain Co., which is said to have been established in 1689. This bowl is typical of its early 20thC products. It is decorated in underglaze blue with large-scale bamboo leaves. Other popular patterns from this factory are irises, chrysanthemums and peonies.
* Occasionally, iron-red is added to the underglaze blue.

* Late 19th and early 20thC wares were made by Esiaiemon Fukagawa, a descendent of the potter who founded the Fragrant Orchid factory in Arita some time after 1879. A superb craftsman, he perfected the use of overglaze and underglaze enamels, producing some exceptionally beautiful pieces that appeared to be virtually three-dimensional. This effect was often heightened by moulding.

41

EUROPEAN PORCELAIN

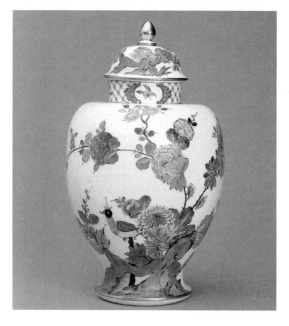

A Meissen vase, made in the early 1730s

For a thousand years after its discovery, porcelain was a mystery in Europe. In the 13thC the traveller Marco Polo described the beautiful porcelain bowls of Fujian; and in the 14th and 15thC a few individual pieces were itemized in aristocratic inventories. However, the Europeans did not attempt to make porcelain themselves until late in the 16thC, after the Portuguese had begun to import it in substantial quantities.

In 1575, Duke Francesco de Medici opened a porcelain factory in Florence. In France, almost a hundred years later, the Poterat family founded a factory in Rouen, and a few years after that a second French factory was established at St Cloud near Paris. In England, as early as 1671, John Dwight of Fulham took out a patent on a porcelain formula, although there is no evidence that he ever made any. But all these porcelains were hybrid soft-pastes. It was not until 1708 that the alchemist Johann Friedrich Böttger produced the first European formula for a true hard-paste porcelain. In the following year, his patron, Augustus the Strong, Elector of Saxony, opened a factory at Meissen, near Dresden, and it has been in production ever since.

From Meissen, the secret formula, or *arcanum*, was spread across Europe by a small handful of venal employees. The first was a former goldsmith, Conrad Hunger, who obtained the formula from Böttger while he was drunk and set out with the kiln-master, Samuel Stölzel, for Vienna, where they helped a court official, Claudius du Paquier, to start Europe's second hard-paste factory. Another Meissen employee, Adam Friedrich Löwenfink, helped to establish a factory at Höchst, and soon afterwards three of the Höchst employees left to help the Duke of Brunswick set up a factory in Fürstenberg. By 1770, there were almost twenty hard-paste factories in Europe, all of them making their own versions of Oriental export porcelain or emulating the shapes of European silverware.

The first Italian hard-paste factory was founded in Venice by another goldsmith, Francesco Vezzi, again with the help of Conrad Hunger. The factory closed around 1727, shortly after Hunger went back to Meissen and arranged to cut off the essential supply of suitable clay from Aue in Saxony. But the Italian hard-paste tradition did not die with the Vezzi factory. In the same year an important factory was established at Doccia, near Florence; and in 1764 another more successful Venetian factory was founded by Geminiano Cozzi. However, the most famous Italian porcelain comes from the soft-paste factory founded in 1743 at Capo di Monte in Naples, where the great modeller Guiseppe Gricci overcame the plasticity of his material to produce some of the most animated and charming of all porcelain figures.

In France, the soft-paste tradition continued for most of the 18thC. Following the foundation of Rouen and St Cloud, the Prince de Condé established a factory at Chantilly and the Duc de Villeroy opened one in Paris which he later moved to Mennecy. In 1756, the eighteen-year-old factory at Vincennes moved to Sèvres, and two years later it was taken over by its principal shareholder, King Louis XV. Protected by sumptuary laws, which among other things prevented other factories from using gilding, the French royal factory prospered. After the Seven Years' War, which ended in 1763, Sèvres took over from Meissen as the leader in European fashion. Five years later the factory acquired a hard-paste formula, and from then until the Revolution, while hard-paste gradually replaced soft-paste, it made magnificent, coloured-ground wares embellished with the finest gilding ever seen on porcelain. Although several hard-paste factories sprang up around Paris after the Revolution, none of them was a match for Sèvres, and for all their quality, their wares differed little in style from the products of Meissen, Berlin or Vienna.

England came comparatively late to the manufacture of porcelain. Chelsea, Bow and Lund's of Bristol did not begin production until the 1740s, although they were soon to be followed by Derby, Longton Hall, Lowestoft and the first hard-paste factory – Plymouth. Apart from Worcester, Lowestoft and Derby, these factories closed or were taken over within little more than a decade, but several of the late 19thC factories, established to make "bone-china" for an expanding middle class market, are still in production.

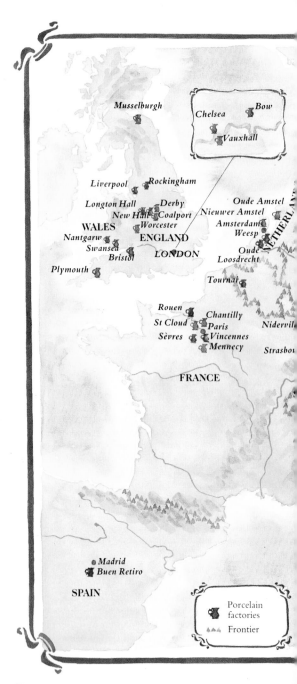

Musselburgh

Chelsea   Bow

Vauxhall

Liverpool   Rockingham

Longton Hall   Derby   Oude Amstel

New Hall Coalport   Nieuwer Amstel

WALES   Worcester   Amsterdam

Nantgarw   ENGLAND   Weesp

Swansea   Oude

Bristol   LONDON   Loosdrecht   NETHERLAND

Plymouth

Tournai

Rouen

St Cloud   Chantilly

Paris

Sèvres   Vincennes   Nidervil

Mennecy

Strasbo

FRANCE

Madrid

Buen Retiro

SPAIN

Porcelain
factories

Frontier

44

Copenhagen

BERLIN
Fürstenberg

Meissen
Dresden
ERMANY
Kloster-Veilsdorf
Höchst

Fulda
Frankenthal
Ludwigsburg
Augsburg   VIENNA
Nymphenburg
Munich   AUSTRIA
rich
RLAND

Le Nove
Este   *Venice*

Vinovo
FLORENCE *Doccia*

ITALY

ROME

Naples

PRINCIPAL EUROPEAN
CENTRES

MEISSEN 1

*A Böttger stoneware silver-mounted tankard
1712-15; ht 4½in/11.5cm; value code B*

Identification checklist for Meissen porcelain and
stoneware before c.1728
1. If the piece is stoneware, is it very close-grained?
2. Has the piece been polished or cut into facets?
3. Is there carved decoration?
4. Is the piece the shape of silverware?
5. If the piece is porcelain, is it hard-paste?
6. Is the glaze warm and creamy?
7. Are there any splits or tears where the paste has
dried out too soon?
8. If the piece is a beaker, does it have the bell-shape
found in *blanc-de-Chine*?
9. Is it decorated with realistic moulded leaves?
10. Are there no identifying marks on it?

Europe's first hard-paste
In Saxony, in the last quarter of
the 17thC, an amateur natural
scientist, Count Ehrenfried
Walter von Tschirnhausen, set
out to find a formula for a true
hard-paste porcelain that could
rival the Chinese imports.
After many years of failure,
the Count's luck changed in
1707 when he acquired the
unwilling assistance of a brilliant
young alchemist from Prussia,
Johann Freidrich Böttger.

**Johann Friedrich Böttger
(1682-1719)**
Böttger had built up such a great
reputation in Prussia that many
people, including King Frederick I,
believed he was on the brink of
discovering a formula for gold.
Fearing rightly that the impecu-
nious king was planning to lock
him up until he succeeded,
Böttger fled to Saxony, where he
was seized for the same purpose
by the elector, Augustus the
Strong. Augustus kept Böttger

46

under guard and forced him to continue his experiments, but in 1707, frustrated by their inevitable failure, he ordered him to stop and assist Tschirnhausen instead. Although the new project was to bring Böttger a level of success and fame that he would never have known as an alchemist, he always regarded it as unworthy of his talents. On the door of his quarters, he wrote "God our creator made a potter out of a gold-maker".

On January 15th, 1708, Böttger and Tschirnhausen recorded a formula for porcelain which proved successful in the first firing. Eager for profit, the elector agreed to found the Royal Saxon Porcelain Factory in his castle at Meissen, where Böttger was being held. In 1710, shortly after the count's death, the new factory began to produce its famous red stoneware, and in 1713 it exhibited Europe's first hard-paste porcelain. In 1714, Böttger was appointed administrator of the factory and formally granted his freedom. By then his health had been ruined by hard work and confinement, and depression had turned him into an alcoholic. On March 13th, 1719, he died at the age of thirty-seven.

Red stoneware
The designs for the stoneware, which Böttger called "Jaspice Ware", were influenced by the former glass-cutters and silversmiths who worked in the factory. Many of the shapes were copied from silverware. The close-grained pottery was so hard that it could be cut like glass.

Some of Böttger's products show the influence of Kakiemon shapes, but these pieces are always decorated and finished in the style of Bohemian cut glass.

Hard-paste porcelain
Böttger's early hard-paste is covered in a warm, milky glaze. Designs were based on stoneware models. Vessels, particularly beakers, often have realistically moulded acanthus leaves around the base.
* Many pieces are split or torn in places where they dried out too soon.

Böttger was influenced by Japanese decorations as well as Japanese shapes. This typical teapot, moulded with acanthus leaves, has been decorated with a Japanese scene in the Kakiemon palette.

The earliest Meissen products were also strongly influenced by Chinese styles. Under Böttger's direction, both stoneware and white-glazed porcelain were used to make "pagoda" figures based on Jingdezhen incense burners, some of which were embellished with gilding and polychrome decoration. Other Chinese influences were *blanc-de-Chine* wares and the red stoneware imported from Yixing, particularly teapots.

Marks
There are no identification marks on the earliest Meissen.

47

MEISSEN 2

A lidded tureen
c.1730; ht 6-7in/15-18cm; value code C

Identification checklist for Meissen wares from 1728-63
1. Is the porcelain hard-paste?
2. Is it close-grained, greyish and a little chalky?
3. Is the mark correct? (see *facing page*)
4. If the base is flat, are there little flecks on the unglazed surface?
5. Are puce and iron-red dominant in the decoration?
6. If there are figures in the decoration, are they standing on a surface of milky green?
7. If the piece is in the Kakiemon style, are the enamels sunk into the porcelain?
8. Do figures depict Orientals or merchants?

Johann Gregor Herold (1696-1775)
The second phase in the history of Germany's first great porcelain factory began in 1720 with the arrival of Johann Gregor Herold, a brilliant painter who had been working at du Paquier's new factory in Vienna. Herold succeeded Böttger as administrator and in 1723, in recognition of his talent, he was appointed court painter to the elector. Under Herold, Meissen wares acquired the exquisite decorations and palette that were to make them famous.

Chinoiserie
Basing his drawings on earlier prints, Herold designed tranquil Oriental scenes.

* The languid, elegant figures are elongated, like figures in fashion plates.
* They stand on terraces supported by gilded Baroque scrollwork, and the whole scene is usually surrounded by a similar Baroque frame.
* Scenes painted before 1725 generally have clouds in the background.

Early palette
* Herold's early designs are dominated by an unnatural combination of iron-red and puce. These dramatic colours were copied by other factories, but the colour that distinguishes Meissen is the rich milky green beneath the figures. Within the scrollwork, there is also a pinkish lustre.

From 1729, the elector allowed the factory to make copies of many of the pieces in his collection of Kakiemon wares. Although these copies were intended to be as close as possible to the originals, there are still noticeable differences:
* The Japanese painting is looser.
* The enamels on Meissen wares have sunk in and lie flush with the surface of the porcelain. On real Kakiemon wares, the enamels lie proud.
* In addition, there is a type of Meissen flower painting which is a mixture of Japanese Kakiemon and Chinese *famille verte*.

Herold was a brilliant colour-chemist as well as a fine painter and imaginative designer. In the late 1720s, he introduced a series of solid coloured grounds which achieved a flawless surface during firing, and the elector, who was by that time a passionate collector of his own products, decorated entire rooms in his palace to match them.
  The most popular of these colours were:
* turquoise (as on this miniature tea caddy)
* imperial, egg-yolk yellow
* pea-green
* strong sea-green
* puce, or claret
* tomato-red.

European decoration
During the 1730s, European themes became more popular than the Oriental patterns. Many of the wares from this period are decorated with flowers or birds, or (as on the tea caddy) landscapes in the manner of painters such as Watteau and Lancret, enclosed in gilt Rococo frames.

The new formula
Meissen porcelain made after about 1725 is very different from the porous variety invented by Böttger. The paste is close-grained, slightly grey and a little chalky; and there are extraneous slivers of clay sticking to the underside of pieces with flat unglazed bases. In addition, the glaze is much smoother and glassier, and it now has the cold, bluish look associated with the factory.

Identification points
* The handles on large vessels are wishbone-shaped with small scrolls at the joints.
* Handles on cups are simple loops with projections at the bottom.
* Pot lids are artichoke-shaped.

Marks

* Rare marks found on some wares after 1724 are the initials KPM (Königliche Porzellan Manufaktur).

* The initials AR (Augustus Rex) are also found on some, usually larger, Kakiemon wares.

* After 1725, the most common mark is the crossed swords in underglaze blue, from the arms of Saxony.

* From 1730 onwards, the angle between the swords becomes noticeably more acute.

* From c.1740 onwards, the mark is smaller – on most pieces it is less than 0.7in (2cm) long.

49

A figure of Harlequin *from the* Commedia dell'Arte
c.1740; ht 7-8in/17.5-20.5cm; value code A

Identification checklist for Meissen figures from 1731-75
1. Are the figures separately modelled?
2. Is the facial expression a bit severe but subtly painted?
3. Is the modelling very detailed?
4. Is the hair finely detailed in black?
5. Does the base have applied flowers or Rococo scrolls?
6. If the mark is not on the base, is it on the back or side?

Monumental figures
In 1730, the Elector Augustus commissioned 910 monumental figures of animals for his new palace. The thick body of the paste made the figures so heavy that many collapsed in the kiln.

Those few that have survived are covered in cracks where the moisture has been driven out in the firing. The enamelling produced so many defects that the figures were eventually left in the white.

Johann Joachim Kändler (1706-1775)

The first monumental figures were very lifeless and unrealistic, but their quality improved dramatically in 1731, after the arrival of a young sculptor called Johann Joachim Kändler, who was to become the greatest of all the porcelain modellers. Although he was never able to overcome the technical problems, Kändler studied the animals in the elector's menagerie and produced life-like and animated figures. When the project ended, shortly after the elector's death in 1733, Kändler applied his talent to designing on a smaller scale. Soon the factory was producing flawless figures to decorate the dinner table, and from around 1740 until Kändler's death in 1775, Meissen figures replaced wares as the most admired and sought-after of the factory's products.

Kändler figures

The faces on Kändler's figures are usually a bit severe, but the colouring is very subtle. Figures in groups are always separate and very detailed. The hair is usually very finely executed with black or dark brown brush strokes. There is so much twisting movement in the modelling that the figures often look as though they are about to topple over.

Subjects

The earliest figures represented ladies and gentlemen of the court and characters from the Italian *Commedia dell'Arte*, including the most popular of all Kändler figures, the series of Harlequins modelled between 1738 and 1744.
  Other sets of figures include:
* peasants in national costume
* shepherds and shepherdesses
* mythological subjects
* *The Cries of Paris*
* *The Cries of London*
* Chinese and Middle Eastern figures
* animals and birds, particularly parrots.

Marks

The earliest Kändler figures were often glazed and marked on the underside. However, by 1740 the bases were usually unglazed and their marks were ground away when flattened. As a result, in the course of the next ten years, it became the custom to paint a very small mark on the back or the side of a figure.

The early figures are set on simple pad bases or on mounds with applied flowers, and their strong colours are painted on in large washes, but the figures made after the late 1740s, such as this one, are dominated by pastel colours and stand on heavier bases decorated with Rococo scrolls.

The pre-eminence of figures at Meissen influenced the design and decoration of the wares. Little figures were used as the knops on the lids of teapots and larger vessels. On this candlestick, made before 1735, an ingenious painter has found room for typical Meissen Chinoiserie decorations amid the overwhelming Baroque moulding.

MEISSEN 4

*A Neo-rococo Meissen dinner service
c.1850; value code A*

Identification checklist for Meissen porcelain after 1774
1. Is the paste smooth, slightly off-white and free from flecks?
2. Is the glaze glassier and somewhat bluer than before? (See pp.46-51.)
3. Are the colours even paler and more washed out than Rococo colours?
4. If the piece is a figure, does it have a slightly concave, glazed base?
5. Is the base of the figure painted overall in brown or tan and edged in gilding?
6. Is the hair pale and in thickish strands?
7. Does the figure have large numbers incised on the base?
8. Is the mark larger than in earlier periods?

Count Marcolini (1774-1814)
In 1774, Marcolini was appointed director of Meissen. Abandoning the Rococo in favour of a severe Neo-classicism, he introduced silhouettes, biscuit figures, classical reliefs in the manner of Wedgwood, and miniature paintings on solid grounds in the styles of Angelica Kaufmann, Nicholas Berchem and Antonio Canaletto. He also created a new fashion for underglaze blue. However, the factory failed to make a profit and he was dismissed in 1813.

Later porcelain

For a time after Marcolini's death the factory continued with Neo-classicism, but in the 1830s it returned to the Rococo in a somewhat debased form. Meissen hardly strayed from this path until the 1920s, when they produced a number of stylish and innovative figures.

This tea and coffee service is painted in the manner of Johann Georg Loehnig with miniatures from *Aesop's Fables*. It was made between 1774 and 1785, but the shapes were introduced c.1750.
* Meissen decorations at this time were among the best ever painted in Europe.
* The wreaths and narrow gilt borders are very typical of early Neo-classical Meissen.

Under Marcolini, Rococo bases were replaced either by circular bases moulded with key fret or plain slab bases such as these.
* The stiff, elongated posture and crisply detailed drapery are characteristic of this period.
* The broad washes of pastel colours were used particularly on classical figures. Contemporary figures were decorated with stripes or tiny florets.

This coffee cup and saucer are painted in fresh and lively enamels with bouquets of summer flowers in a debased form of *deutsche Blumen*. At this stage, the dominant colour is pale pink rather than puce, and the painting is more romantic and less academic.
* The broad band of gilding and the grooved, rectilinear handle are typical of wares produced by Marcolini.

Like many wares from the late 19thC, this cabinet plate is painted in an earlier style, in this case after Angelica Kauffmann.
* Like other factories, Meissen covered the whole surface with the subject, rather than confining it to a small reserve, but it was the only factory to use this border.

Marks

The crossed swords of the Marcolini period are larger and longer than on earlier products. They have a star between the hilts, and sometimes the Roman numerals I or II have been added below.
* After Marcolini the star was no longer used.
* From the early 19thC onwards, the bases of figures are incised with large cursive numbers and stamped with small serif numbers.

Many of Meissen's 19thC revivals of 18thC figures, such as this, have clumsy Rococo bases and rather washed out tones, which contrast dramatically with the sharper delineation and bolder colours of the 18thC.

HAUSMALER

A Böttger Hausmaler *coffee pot, decorated by Abraham Seuter*
1725-30; ht10in/25.4cm; value code C/D

Identification checklist for *Hausmaler* porcelain
1. Is the porcelain Meissen?
2. Is the piece decorated in monochrome?
3. Is the decoration a bit too large-scale for the vessel?
4. Is the piece completely decorated in Chinoiserie gilding? (Seuter)
5. Is the overglaze decoration incompatible with the underglaze decoration? (Ferner)
6. Are there birds or flowers on the rim? (Meyer)

Hausmaler
Some of the finest painting to be found on any German porcelain was caried out by independent *hausmalerei* (home painters) who, even in the early days of Böttger, bought wares in the white from the Meissen factory and decorated them in enamel or gilt in their own studios and workshops.
* Most of these wares were either plates or tea and coffee services, and as the blanks were mainly bought in bulk, many of them were kept in store and not decorated until up to ten years after they were made.

Abraham Seuter (1688-1747)

The most prolific of the recognizable *hausmalerei* were Abraham Seuter and his brother Bartholomaus, who ran a workshop in Augsburg. Their finest decorations are gilt Chinoiserie silhouettes set on elaborate scrolled and trellised consoles.

* Although flat, the figures in these scenes are highlighted with chiselled details.
* The Seuters almost always used borders composed of small cogged, or toothed, scrolls.
* Much of their work was carried out on unmarked Böttger porcelain dating from around 1720.

Franz Ferdinand Meyer, who worked in Bohemia from the late 1740s to the 1770s, was an extremely prolific decorator. Most of his output seems to have been on plates marked with crossed swords, which he painted with hunting scenes and landscapes after Göz, a German engraver, using a fairly subdued palette.
* Meyer often painted birds, flowers or elaborate gilt scrolls on the rims of the plates.

Perhaps the most painterly of the *hausmalerei* was Sabina Auffenwerth, who is also known by her married name, Hosenestel. She usually painted Meissen-style Chinoiseries or else relatively large scale contemporary figures, such as those on this chocolate cup and saucer, painted c.1730.
* As in the cup and saucer, Auffenwerth often used monochrome black, purple or red and then highlighted the faces and arms in strong flesh tones.
* Her gilding, which is more ambitious than Seuter's, is composed of a combination of intricate trellis panels and loose strapwork, in which she sometimes incorporated her monogram.

Johann Georg Heintze painted landscapes at Meissen until 1742, but his *hausmaler* work is much more wide-ranging, and includes classical subjects such as this.

Ignaz Preissler, the son of a famous glass-decorator, painted in the manner of glass enamelling. Most of his work was in monochrome red or, as here, *Schwarzlot*. His favourite subjects were town- and landscapes, hunting and battle scenes, mythological scenes and Chinoiseries surrounded by Baroque *Laub und Bandelwerk*.

E. J. Ferner, one of the less accomplished *hausmaler*, sometimes added "wooden" figures to old underglaze blue Meissen.

Other decorators

Other important *hausmalerei* were:
* J. F. Metz, who painted Chinoiserie, birds and flowers
* Canon A. O. E. von dem Busch, who engraved porcelain as a hobby.

VIENNA 1

A du Paquier ollientopfe, *or pot*
c.1725; ht 7in/17.8cm; value code D (lid missing) C (with lid)

Identification checklist for du Paquier porcelain
1. Is the porcelain hard-paste?
2. Is the glaze thin and slightly green?
3. Is the piece made in a mixture of styles?
4. Are the reserves in the decoration shaped like Chinese lanterns?
5. Do the scenes in the decoration have a deep perspective?
6. Does the decoration contain latticework with little star-like flowers at the intersections?
7. Does it also include moulded *fleurs-de-lis*?
8. Is it in monochrome?
9. If the piece is a figure, is it somewhat awkward and lacking in detail?

Du Paquier (1718-44)
Europe's second porcelain factory was founded in Vienna by Claudius Innocentius du Paquier. In 1717, after several years of unsuccessful experiment, he bribed one of the Meissen decorators, Christoph Konrad Hunger, to come to Vienna and teach him Böttger's formula, and in the following year he was granted a 25-year monopoly by the Austrian emperor, Charles VI. When it became obvious that Hunger did not know as much as he pretended, du Paquier offered a much larger inducement to the Meissen arcanist Samuel Stölzel. Stölzel did not stay long in Vienna. In 1720, frustrated by du Paquier's failure to pay him, he went back to Meissen accompanied by his best painter, Johann Gregor Herold.

But by then du Paquier had his secret, and the Vienna factory was producing porcelain. In time, du Paquier was to lose the secret as easily as he had gained it. One of his painters, Joseph Jakob Ringler, won his daughter's affections and persuaded her to help him obtain the formula, which he in turn took on to Höchst, Frankenthal, Ludwigsburg and Ellwangen.

Hard-paste
Inevitably, the greyish-white Vienna hard-paste is very like the Meissen paste, although it is sometimes slightly bluer and smokier.
* However, the glaze, which has a slightly green tone, is not so similar. In general it is much thinner and less glassy than on Meissen.

Style

Du Paquier's porcelain reflected the grandeur and exuberance of a Baroque city. His shapes are much more original than those produced at Meissen, and their solidity contrasts dramatically with his delicate and often very different decorations. The three-footed *ollientopfe* in the main picture, which was made for a Spanish stew called *ollia*, reflects a typical mixture of influences:-

* the masked feet are from silverware
* the flower-like shape of the rim is Japanese
* the stiff, wandering design is painted in the Chinese *famille verte* palette.

In addition, the square handles are very common on du Paquier wares made before 1730.

Du Paquier's *Laub und Bandelwerk* (leaf and strapwork), which was initially used to decorate borders, gradually evolved into complex but delicate geometric patterns. Latticework filled the reserves, and tiny star-like flowers were added at its junctions. On this vase, which was made around 1725, the puce and iron-red palette could have been Meissen, but the decoration and the moulded *fleurs-de-lis* could not be anything but du Paquier.

Schwarzlot

Many of du Paquier's wares were decorated in monochrome, particularly black, which was known as *Schwarzlot*. The designs were usually copied directly from engravings of birds, animals and landscapes.

This baluster vase, which is over 20in/50.8cm tall, is perhaps one of the most ambitious pieces ever made by du Paquier. It has many of the features which distinguish his wares from the Meissen equivalents:-

* where Meissen would have used an Oriental shape, du Paquier has taken a European silverware shape and decorated it with an Oriental design
* the palette seems similar, but here it is warmer and there is a much greater predominance of the Rococo puce
* the reserves have a Chinese lantern shape which was unique to the Vienna factory
* the figures and landscapes within the reserves have a much deeper perspective
* although there is more gilt than usual on a du Paquier piece, it has still been used comparatively sparingly.

Du Paquier made only a few figures, most of which were Chinese or *Commedia dell'Arte* characters, such as *Colombine* and *Pantaloon, above*. Small and stiff with slightly awkward stances, they lack movement and have none of the detail of later models.

* *Pantaloon's* coat has been painted in silver-oxide, which, although often used in Japan, was rarely used in Europe.

Marks

There are no marks on du Paquier products.

VIENNA 2

Vienna figures
c.1760-70; ht 8in/20.3cm; value code E each

Identification checklist for Vienna porcelain, 1744-84
1. Is the porcelain hard-paste and greyish?
2. Is the glaze white and glassy?
3. Do the shapes of the wares follow Meissen or, if not, are they decorated in Imari colours?
4. If a hollow figure, is it without a base?
5. If the figure has a mound base, does it look as though it has been hacked with a knife?
6. Is the base decorated with a triangular gilt pattern?
7. Does the figure have a mark accompanied by incised numbers and letters?

Vienna, from 1744-84

In 1744, du Paquier allowed his factory to be taken over by the Austrian state, which had been lending him money for several years. Under State management, which lasted until 1784, Vienna continued to produce many of du Paquier's shapes and patterns and introduced new Rococo table wares in the manner of Meissen. Many of these were decorated by some of the best enamellers of the day, including Johann Gottfried Klinger, who came from Meissen in 1746 and stayed until his death in 1781. By far the most important products during the "State" period were the figures, especially those by Johann Joseph

Niedermayer, who served as master modeller from 1747-84.

Paste and glaze

From 1749 onwards the Vienna factory used a much finer clay, which was imported from Hungary, but the paste is still slightly grey. The State period glaze is white but glassy.

Palette

By far the most dominant colours, particularly on the figures, are green and pale mauve or lilac, but three other colours are also prominent:
* puce
* lemon yellow
* egg-yolk yellow.

The *putti, above right,* modelled by
J. J. Niedermayer, c.1760-65,
although charming, seems lifeless
compared to the Frankenthal
figure by J. W. Lanz, *above left.*

This hunter is typical of State
period figures. Although there is a
hint of movement, the posture is
on the whole slightly stiff. There
is not a great deal of detailing in
the modelling of State figures, and
the full-cheeked faces with
blushed cheeks and strongly
rouged lips have very little
character.

Bases
In the 1760s, the Rococo bases
were replaced by almost pie-
shaped pads which look as though
they have been hacked with a
knife. Some, like those in the
main picture, are washed in greens
and browns, and many, like the
hunter's, have triangular patterns
picked out in gilt round the edge.

Under du Paquier and in the early
State period, the Vienna factory
produced a number of Imari
wares, using late 17th or early
18thC designs from Japan. The
potters and painters went to
unusual lengths to replicate the
original, even adding blue to the
glaze, but the painting is much
more mechanical.

This teapot, c.1750-55, is a typical
Vienna anachronism. Based on a
Meissen shape from 30 years
earlier, it is decorated in the
manner of J. G. Herold, but is
angular and heavily modelled, and
the overall effect is much less
balanced than that of the original.

Some early State period Vienna
figures are without bases. This
Dutch peasant comes from a
series attributed to Ludwig van
Lücke, who was at Vienna 1750-52.

Marks
During the State period, the Vienna
factory adopted the Austrian shield
as its mark. Figures also have
impressed numbers and letters for
the decorators and repairers.

VIENNA 3

A Vienna jardinière, painted by Joseph Nigg
c.1817; ht 17¾in/45cm; value code A/B

Identification checklist for Vienna wares, 1784-1864
1. Is the porcelain hard-paste?
2. Do wares have three impressed date numerals?
3. Is the shape Neo-classical?
4. Does the decoration cover all the exterior porcelain?
5. Is the gilding very high quality with matt and burnished surface details?
6. Can you feel the gilding?
7. Does the piece have more than one coloured ground?
8. Is it decorated with classical subjects in the manner of Angelica Kaufmann or painted with realistic and large-scale flowers?
9. Are you sure that the mark is not printed? (There were a number of imposters after the closure of the factory.)

Vienna, from 1784-1864
In 1784, when the factory had got into such serious financial difficulties that it was unsaleable, Konrad Sorgel von Sorgenthal was appointed director. He abandoned the Rococo and embraced Neo-classicism completely, especially the Sèvres style, with solid coloured grounds and sumptuous gilt scrollwork. Several ground colours, including a dark blue and a claret, were developed by Joseph Leithner for the factory. Also in tune with Sèvres, a number of biscuit porcelain figures and busts were introduced. Although Sorgenthal died in 1805, the factory continued to use and develop his innovations until its closure in 1864.

Paste and glaze
At a time when the finest European porcelains appeared very similar, Vienna was subtly

different. It was sometimes warmer and not as glassy as Berlin, Paris and Meissen.

Wares
Under Sorgenthal, Vienna's success depended on its richly gilded services and tea and coffee wares, and its decorative wares, in which surface modelling was restricted.
* The gilding of this period is heavy and three-dimensional – a feature which was much copied by other factories in the late 19thC.

This solitaire coffee set, made in 1821, is archetypal of the heavy Biedermeier-style with which Vienna is closely associated. The central oval panels are sensitively painted with classical semi-erotic subjects by Johann Geyer in the manner of Angelica Kaufmann.
* The complex borders with alternating registers of gilding and solid colour epitomize the Vienna style which other factories sought to copy.
* The straight-sided vessels with concave shoulders are also typical.

Figures
The few figures made in this period were usually classical and almost always biscuit. The most common subjects were:-
* busts of the imperial family and famous figures, such as Haydn
* groups from Pompeian paintings
* copies of classical statues.

This solitaire coffee set, with a pierced oval tray, is decorated *en grisaille* with fantastic animals and classical subjects, in a style very similar to contemporary Paris and Sèvres. However, the shapes are

purely Vienna, with high, looped and pierced handles and three raised scroll feet.
* There are two coloured grounds – pink and a bronze-lustre. The bronze-lustre is believed to have been invented at the factory during the period of Sorgenthal's management.

The botanical painting on Vienna porcelain is among the very best of the Neo-classical period. The tray on this service is brilliantly painted, probably by Joseph Nigg, who was one of the great painters at the factory and in the first rank of all botanical painters.
* The vessels, in the Etruscan style, are decorated in solid gilding delicately highlighted with light tooling.
* Other wares produced at Vienna – as at all the leading factories during this period – include "named view" plates with topographical scenes painted in minute detail.

This ice-pail, with the impress date of 1804, is painted in the "Etruscan" style in iron-red and white with classical subjects. In keeping with the restricted classical palette, it is decorated in only two colours with the addition of gilding.

FRANKENTHAL WARES

A Frankenthal dinner service
1759-62; ht of tureens 13 1/2 in/34cm; value code A

Identification checklist for Frankenthal wares
1. Is the porcelain hard-paste?
2. Is it fine and white?
3. Is the glaze creamy or slightly grey and a bit grainy?
4. Is the piece the shape of silverware?
5. Do the cups have flared mouthrims?
6. Do the plates have basketweave borders?
7. If a pot, is the cover flush with the body of the vessel?
8. Is the decoration Chinoiserie?
9. Are the figures in the decoration larger than on other wares?
10. Do the figures have more movement than on other wares?
11. Is there a lot of gilding?
12. Is the mark right (see p. 65)?

Frankenthal (1755-94)

In 1751, Paul-Antoine Hannong began to manufacture hard-paste porcelain at his faïence factory in Strasbourg. He was so successful that in 1753 King Louis XV, the principal shareholder in the rival soft-paste factory at Vincennes, ordered him to stop. Undaunted, Hannong moved to Frankenthal in the Palatinate, where the Elector Karl Theodor leased him part of an empty barracks and granted him a monopoly. By late 1755, the new figures and table wares were ready for sale.

Paste and glaze

Early Frankenthal porcelain is composed of a fine, white hard-paste, but the quality declined after 1774, when a cheaper clay was introduced.

The well-fused, creamy or slightly grey glaze is opaque and a bit more grainy, or "musliny", than the glaze on other contemporary German products. The glaze is also unusual in that it absorbs the enamel colours, giving the porcelain the overall effect of soft-paste, rather than resistant hard-paste.

Wares

Early Frankenthal wares follow the styles that Paul-Antoine Hannong brought with him from France (see p. 62). The shapes are those of silverware of the period, and there are small, framed areas of decoration amid the mouldings on the rims.
* In general, tea and coffee services have plain bowled cups with subtly flared mouth rims. Handles are usually plain loops with lower terminals shaped like acanthus leaves, or else exaggerated "C" scrolls with reversed curved brackets, similar to those of Fürstenberg.
* A rarer type of cup follows the Meissen quatrelobed design with an angular wishbone handle. The larger tea and coffee vessels and plates are often moulded with basketweave borders.
* Some dinner plates are moulded with floral garlands or wreaths in the manner of the Meissen Gotzkowsky pattern.

These pieces from a *Goldchinesien* tea and coffee service, dated 1772, are typical of the later Frankenthal shapes.

The round-bodied teapot with an ear-shaped handle is borrowed from the *théière calabre* of Sèvres. The coffee pot is basically similar in shape to the pots from Nymphenburg, but it has a thicker neck and it is not so elegant. The pots have no flanges, and covers are flush with the bodies.

Decoration

The most usual decorative themes on Frankenthal wares are:
* landscapes with classical ruins, either supported on gilt Rococo scrollwork or with loose pendant foliage
* *fêtes galantes* after Watteau
* figure subjects in the manner of Boucher
* delicate flower painting in the manner of *deutsche Blumen* but with a much more expansive French technique, and with delicate outspread tendrils in the style of Strasbourg (see p. 62)
* birds in branches in the Berlin style
* Chinoiserie.

Chinoiserie decorations are very rare on 18thC wares from any factory other than Frankenthal. The decorations on this exquisite polychrome cup and saucer, like those on the service shown on the previous page, contain three elements which are typical of the factory:
* The figures are painted on a much larger scale than they are on wares from other factories.
* There is more humour in the subjects and much more movement in the figures.
* The gilding is extensive – unfettered by the French sumptuary laws, which prevented all French factories from employing gilding. The Frankenthal artists used it liberally.

Palette

The Frankenthal palette is much like that of other contemporary factories, although in this case, at least during the 1760s, the dominant colours are green and purple. The other most important colours are:
* puce
* yellowish green
* greyish yellow
* ultramarine
* greyish blue
* chestnut brown

FRANKENTHAL FIGURES

A Frankenthal group of a hunter at the kill, by J.W. Lanz c.1760; ht 7-8in/17.7-20.3cm; value code C/D

Identification checklist for Frankenthal figures
1. Is the porcelain hard-paste?
2. Is the glaze creamy, thin and opaque?
3. Is the figure stiffly modelled?
4. Is the modelling quite detailed?
5. Are the features small and doll-like?
6. Are the hands oversized?
7. Does the figure have an undulating base with gilt or puce scrolls on it?
8. Does the base have arched edges?
9. Are there tufts of green moss on the base?

J.A. Hannong (1734-c.1800)
In 1759, Paul-Antoine Hannong sold the Frankenthal factory to his son Joseph-Adam, and the Elector Karl Theodor agreed to a transfer of its monopolies and privileges. Joseph-Adam was an even better administrator than his father. He immediately enlarged the factory and began to export his wares throughout Europe. But when his father died soon afterwards, his spendthrift brother Pierre-Antoine stole the secret hard-paste formula and sold it to the soft-paste factory at Sèvres in order to pay off his debts. The legal battles that followed depleted Frankenthal's financial resources and distracted Joseph-Adam from its management. In 1762, the Elector Karl Theodor bought out the factory in order to save it. But in 1794, the factory was closed and the moulds were moved to Nymphenburg.

Figures

Frankenthal figures are among the best made in Germany. They are invariably stiffly modelled, but have an undeniable, doll-like charm, with small, innocent features, big eyes, rouged cheeks and oversized hands. The plasticity of Frankenthal porcelain allowed for quite detailed modelling, and the thin, opaque glaze does not obscure it.

Modellers

The first chief modeller at Frankenthal was Johann Wilhelm Lanz, who accompanied Paul-Antoine Hannong from Strasbourg. Lanz modelled all the fashionable subjects, but his favourites were scenes from country life, such as the hunting group on the previous page. His Strasbourg models mainly had grassy mound bases, but at Frankenthal Lanz introduced an undulating Rococo base with puce or gilt scrolls and arched edges that curl like wet paper.

Towards the end of the 1750s Lanz was joined by Johann Frederick Lück, who had previously worked at Höchst. Lück followed Lanz's style, although some of his figures, such as the group *above*, had even more elaborate bases with deeply arched and pierced scrollwork.
* Lück's cousin Karl Gottlieb joined the factory in 1756 and made a wide range of Rococo figures, including some amusing but not very convincing Oriental musicians.
* The great J. P. Melchior also joined the factory in 1779. Now influenced by Neo-classicism, he turned his children into *putti*; and many of his figures were so flawless that they were sold unpainted in marble-like biscuit.

In 1762, after the Elector had bought the factory, the court sculptor, Konrad Linck, was appointed chief modeller. Linck introduced the first hints of Neo-classicism to the factory's style. His own style had an expansiveness which compares with the best of the later work of Kändler; and the sculptural qualities which he applied to his classical figures influenced his other models as well. For example, on this boy with an oboe, the clothes seem sculpted rather than modelled, and the stripes on the breeches are typical of the Neo-classical taste.
* Linck modified the traditional factory base, retaining the undulation and the Rococo scrolls but making it more of a simple brown mound and adding little tufts of green moss.

Marks

The marks on Frankenthal wares and figures are varied:
* From 1755-56 the mark was "PH" for Paul Hannong, sometimes followed by a lion rampant and the quartered chequered shield of the Palatinate in blue.
* From 1759-62 the letters JAH were used, for Joseph-Adam Hannong.
* Another mark, used throughout the history of the factory, was the monogram of the elector beneath a crown.

* Between 1770 and 1788 the last two numerals of the date were added to the monogram, generally below it.

HÖCHST WARES

A Höchst teapot
c.1755; wdth 7¼in/18cm; value code E/F

Identification checklist for Höchst wares
1. Is the porcelain hard-paste?
2. Does it have a glassy and creamy-white glaze similar to *faïence* (see p. 179)?
3. Is the material generally free from flaws?
4. Is there a predominance of green and puce in the colour scheme?
5. Is the piece marked with a wheel (see *opposite*)?
6. If it is a Rococo teapot, is it bullet-shaped with a knop in the form of a closed bud?
7. Does the pot have a wishbone handle with two projecting thumb-pieces?
8. Do cups and bowls have slightly outcurved rims?

Höchst (1750-96)

In 1736, after completing his apprenticeship as a porcelain painter at Meissen, Adam Friedrich von Löwenfink ran away, leaving behind him considerable debts and riding a valuable horse which belonged to his neighbourhood baker. After working for a few years at the *faïence* factories in Bayreuth, Ansbach and Fulda, he followed his future wife to Mainz; and in 1746, with financial backing from two Frankfurt merchants, he obtained permission from the Elector Emmerich Joseph von Breidenbach to open a porcelain factory at Höchst.

The factory did not produce porcelain in any quantity until 1750, after the arrival of the arcanist Joseph Jakob Ringler from Vienna, and by then von Löwenfink had gone. Jealous of his considerable talent for fanciful Oriental decoration, the factory's first painter, Georg Friedrich Hess, had induced the shareholders to dismiss him, and von Löwenfink had gone to Strasbourg, where the owner of the *faïence* factory, Paul-Antoine Hannong, had appointed him manager of his subsidiary at Hagueneau.

Despite the quality of its products, the factory was never financially secure. It was saved from bankruptcy in 1778, when the elector took it over, but the decline continued and in 1796 it was closed down and the moulds were sold.

Hard-paste

Höchst hard-paste porcelain is pure white, generally free from flaws and covered in a glassy, dead white or creamy glaze, which sometimes looks almost like a highly refined *faïence*.

Wares

The Höchst factory followed contemporary fashions, producing useful and decorative wares in the Rococo style, or in the Neo-classical style. As with the other leading German factories, its products are distinguished by subtle characteristics rather than any originality of style.
* Höchst wares usually have neat incised numbers or letters inside the base identifying the workmen.

Design

Tea and coffee wares usually have relatively plain surfaces.
* Teapots in the early Rococo style are a compact "bullet" shape (see previous page). Their lids are recessed into the body, and the knops are often moulded in the form of a closed bud. Their handles, which are in the shape known as "wishbone", have two projecting thumb pieces and lower scroll terminals.
* Cups and teabowls have slightly outcurved rims. The handles on the cups are plain loops, again with scrolled terminals.
* Before 1765, the factory also produced little quatrefoil dishes and helmet shaped jugs with "J"-shaped handles.

Many wares are decorated with landscape cameos in polychrome, puce or green. On some, such as this tea caddy, painted c.1760, the landscape is framed by delicate gilt cartouches. On others the frame is composed of rockwork. Other decorative themes include:
* *deutsche Blumen* flowers
* Chinoiseries
* rustic scenes in the 17thC style of the Teniers
* figure subjects
* battle scenes
* hunting scenes
* Watteauesque *fêtes galantes*.

The standard of painting on Höchst wares is very high. Among the best artists were the founder's brother, Christian Wilhelm von Löwenfink, the painter Johann Zeschinger, who left for Fürstenberg with the modeller Simon Feilner in 1753, Joseph Philipp Danhofer and Joseph Angele, who in 1780 painted the plate *above top*, and *above bottom* (detail only).The wreaths and rectangular frames surrounding scenes from classical mythology are pure Neo-classical, but the Rococo style still dominates, particularly in the puce scale pattern and gilt scrolls on the rim, *above, top*.

The Höchst mark is a wheel taken from the arms of Mainz. Until c.1765 it was painted in overglaze colours, usually red, puce or purple. After that the mark was generally drawn in a greyish underglaze blue. The example *left* is far more common that that on the *right*.

HÖCHST FIGURES

A Höchst group of Slumber Disturbed *modelled by J. P. Melchior
c.1770; ht 5 ⁷/₈ in/15cm; value code E/F*

Identification checklist for Höchst figures
1. Is the porcelain hard-paste?
2. Is the material generally free from flaws?
3. Is the figure painted in pastel shades?
4. Does it have childlike features?
5. If a group, are the figures gathered around fantastic rock- or trelliswork?
6. Is the figure set on a high Rococo-scroll base or a grassy knoll?
7. Are there incised marks on the base?

Johann Peter Melchior (1742-1825)

The products which contributed more than any others to the reputation of the Höchst factory were the models of Johann Peter Melchior. Melchior did not model fashionable ladies and gentlemen or characters from the *Commedia dell'Arte*. Instead, clearly influenced by the philosophy of Jean Jacques Rousseau and the painting of François Boucher, he concentrated on humorous or melancholy pastoral models of peasants at work, pedlars and travelling musicians. But above all he made sentimental models of children, which, like the one in the main picture, were always decorated in pastel shades. His eye for detail and his ability to recreate a mood set him among the greatest modellers, beside Kändler and Bustelli.

The orphaned son of impoverished German peasants, Melchior was apprenticed to a sculptor in Düsseldorf and worked briefly in several French and German cities before arriving at Höchst in 1765 at the age of twenty-three. Two years later he became master modeller; and as his reputation spread, the Elector appointed him court sculptor to prevent other princes from enticing him away. He became a favourite at court, where he formed a friendship with the poet Goethe. But popularity brought envious enemies. When the Elector died, the factory managers reduced his wages, and in 1779 he moved on to the Frankenthal factory (see pp. 64-5).

One of Feilner's contemporaries was Johann Friedrich Lück, who moved on to Frankenthal in 1757. The scrolled bases on these Rococo dancers, decorated in puce and gold, are obvious precursors of the elaborate bases that made Lück famous.

Like this pair of hunters, the rare models from the earliest years at Höchst are very static and painted in strong colours. They have none of the movement, complexity, romanticism and subtle colouring that were to make the later models so distinctive.

Melchior's predecessor as master modeller was Laurentius Russinger, who modelled mostly Chinoiserie figures and groups such as this. Like Melchior's children *opposite*, the group is characteristically set on a mound base with grass and earth detailed in tan and green. The plump, pink faces are typical of the factory.

Marks
The wheel mark on Höchst figures is often accompanied by incised letters or numbers like those shown *above*, some of which were probably used to identify the workman who "repaired" or assembled the figure from its parts.

The first important modeller at Höchst was Simon Feilner, who worked there only briefly at the beginning of his career, before moving on to Fürstenberg in 1753. Feilner modelled a series of *Commedia dell'Arte* figures on pedestals as well as a number of extravagant Rococo groups. This group, showing a young man lying down to look up a girl's skirt as she washes at a fountain, is typical of his early work. The decoration on top of the fountain is typical – each group is set in front of fantastic rockwork or trelliswork – and the whole composition is set on a boldly-scrolled base.

Copies
The wheel mark is not conclusive proof that a figure is Höchst. After it closed, the mark was used by the other factories which successively acquired its moulds. These include Damm, which made *faïence* copies of some of the Melchior models in the late 19thC, and Poppelsdorf and Passau, which made porcelain copies at the beginning of the 20thC.

LUDWIGSBURG WARES

*A Ludwigsburg teapot,
c.1765; ht 5 1/2 in/13cm; value code E.*

Identification checklist for Ludwigsburg wares
1. Is the piece hard-paste?
2. Is the glaze smoky?
3. If the piece is a teapot, is it bullet-shaped with a fruit knop and a flush or recessed cover?
4. Is the mouth of the spout shaped like a bird's head?
5. If the piece is a cup, does it have a C-shaped scroll handle with shell or feather thumb-pieces?
6. If the piece is a saucer, is it quite flared?
7. If the decoration is a landscape, are there two or three tufts of foliage hanging from its base?
8. Is the piece moulded with an overall scale diaper, a band of basketweave, or a frieze of rectangular panels?
9. Is the mark right? (See *facing page.*)

Ludwigsburg (1758/9-1824)
Like many German factories, Ludwigsburg was an aristocratic status symbol. At first a *faïence* factory, it was converted to the manufacture of porcelain by Carl Eugen, Duke of Württemberg, who regarded such a factory as "a necessary attribute of the glory and dignity" of a prince. His first director was J. J. Ringler who had already brought the secret of porcelain to Höchst, Strasbourg and Nymphenburg.

Paste and glaze
The greyish-white, close-grained body is almost entirely obscured by the glaze, which can often be very smoky.
* In general appearance, Ludwigsburg porcelain is very similar to that of Zürich, although the glaze is not quite as glassy.

Teapots
Teapots are usually bullet-shaped and have a recessed or flush cover with a fruit-shaped knop. As on the example *above*, the spouts have mouths shaped like birds or dragons.

Cups
All Ludwigsburg cups, whether plain or moulded, have C-shaped scroll handles with protruding thumb-pieces which are shaped like tiny shells or feathers. Most of them also have dark brown or enamel rims.

Saucers
Unlike the rounded saucers which were made at most of the other German factories, the Ludwigsburg saucers are quite flared, which gave them a tendency to warp in the firing.

As Carl Eugen and his courtiers were always Ludwigsburg's most important customers, its products reflected the tastes of the court even more than the other German factories. In the mid-1760s, when this flared beaker vase was made, there was a widespread fashion among the German aristocracy for grotesque and sentimental depictions of dwarves. Like this example, the most popular designs were based on the engravings of the French artist Jacques Callot.
* The vase, based on a Chinese shape, has Ludwigsburg's typical smoky glaze and warm palette, which has even been used on the rather florid complexions of the two dwarves.

Other decorative themes
Apart from landscapes, the most common Ludwigsburg designs are:
* *fêtes galantes* after Watteau or Lancret, showing wooden, puppet-like figures painted in silky puce, deep russet and frosty, greyish blue
* birds, which are usually much truer to life than on wares from other German factories
* fruit and flowers in the manner of Meissen.

Marks
The standard mark in use between 1758 and 1793 is a ducal crown above a pair of interlaced Cs – the cipher of Carl Eugen. This mark can be confused with the mark of Niderviller, but the Niderviller mark is usually much more loosely executed. Other, rarer marks include:
* a royal crown over the initials FR or WR, for Kings Frederick and William, respectively
* the stag's antlers from the arms of Württemberg, either as a single set or alternatively, in a group of three.

Most marks are drawn in underglaze blue, but there are also a few which have been gilded or drawn in iron-red or black. On a very small number of pieces the mark has been impressed into the body.

The band of fine basketweave on this bowl is typical of moulded Ludwigsburg wares. Other moulded wares have either an overall scale diaper, or else a narrow frieze of unconnected rectangular panels with beaded borders surrounding formal feathery scrolls. Also typical is the unframed landscape painted in a gloomy autumnal palette, in which dark brown, dirty yellow and green predominate.
Following the German tradition, Ludwigsburg landscapes have romantic architecture in the background and small, stick-like figures in the foreground. However, they also have two or three tufts of foliage around the base – a device that is only seen elsewhere on Fürstenberg wares and the work of Fidèle Duvivier at Worcester.

LUDWIGSBURG FIGURES

A Ludwigsburg Chinoiserie group, modelled by J. Weinmuller c.1770; ht 13¾in/38.5cm; value code C

Identification checklist for Ludwigsburg figures
1. Is the piece hard-paste?
2. Is the glaze a smoky grey colour?
3. Is the piece stiff but crisply modelled?
4. Is it decorated in subdued pastel shades?
5. Is the face characterless?
6. If a miniature, is it an animated and brightly painted group?
7. Is the mark right? (see *previous page*)

Ludwigsburg figures
The first director of Ludwigsburg was Joseph Jakob Ringler, who stole the secret formula for porcelain from his first employer, the Vienna factory. After selling his knowledge at Höchst, Strasbourg and Nymphenburg, he came to Ludwigsburg in 1759 and remained there as director until 1802.

Ringler was accompanied by Gottlieb Friedrich Riedel, who had previously been director of painting at Frankenthal. Riedel had been responsible for some of Frankenthal's most exuberant Rococo wares, but at Ludwigsburg he was to influence the creation of more restrained and elegant Rococo figures.

These figures are undoubtedly the finest of Ludwigsburg's products. Although occasionally naïve, they are crisply modelled and precisely decorated in pastel colours which blend with the smoky tone of the glaze.

Some of the best were modelled by the architect, painter and court sculptor Johann Christian

Wilhelm Beyer, who was overseer of the modelling workshop from about 1764 to 1767. In the 1790s several models were made by the great Neo-classical sculptor Johann Heinrich von Dannecker, but by then the factory was in decline. Although it underwent a brief revival at the beginning of the following century, it closed in 1824.

Palette
The principal colours in Ludwigsburg's restrained Rococo palette are:
* greyish puce
* greyish cobalt
* greyish green
* yellow
* iron-red
* mid-brown
* black
* gilding.

Bases
There is a surprising variety of bases on Ludwigsburg figures; these range from simple grass or rockwork mounds and slabs, highlighted in washed out green or russet, to expensive and complicated Rococo compositions with deeply moulded "C"-scrolls picked out in gilding.

The miniature groups are among the most famous of all the Ludwigsburg figures. The first series, designed by Riedel, represented scenes from the Venetian fair which was held annually by the duke and his court following the duke's visit to Italy in 1767. This was followed by groups by Beyer representing daily life, such as this tavern scene and group of cobblers.
* Although less than $3^{1}/_{2}$ in/8.8 cm in height, these groups are much more animated than the larger figures.

Ballets and masques were the height of fashion in the mid-18thC, and as with the decorations on its wares, Ludwigsburg's figures often reflected the interests of the courtiers. This pair was modelled between 1760 and 1765 by Joseph Nees, under the direction of G. F. Riedel.
* The figures are a little stiff and do not seem to "grow" out of their base, but the decoration is typically restrained – most of the surface has been left in the white – and the characteristically crisp modelling can be seen on the girl's sharply pleated skirt.
* On areas that have been left in the white, the smoky Ludwigsburg glaze gives the porcelain the look of marble, and the well-defined limbs often look as though they have been carved.

This lively group was modelled by Johann Jacob Louis, who was chief repairer at Ludwigsburg and also assistant to Riedel. It represents a scene from a comic story involving a court tailor, his wife and a goat and is considerably more animated and light-hearted than the version which was produced at Meissen, but, as on most Ludwigsburg figures, the faces are characterless.
* The upper part of the base is typically mottled in subdued greens and tans.

NYMPHENBURG WARES

A pair of Nymphenburg plates
c.1760/5; dia. approx 9in/23cm; value code D

Identification checklist for Nymphenburg wares
1. Is the porcelain hard-paste?
2. Is it free of imperfections?
3. Is the glaze a greyish colour, but a greenish-cream in places where it has pooled (see *opposite page*)?
4. Is the piece marked with an impressed shield?
5. Is the decoration particularly skilfully and sensitively painted?
6. Does it represent birds on branches or loose bouquets of flowers?
7. If the piece is a tea cup, does it have complex, ear-shaped handles?
8. If the piece is a teapot, is it shaped like a truncated pear, with a swan's head spout and a tube projecting from its beak?

Nymphenburg (1747-present)
In 1747, the Elector Max Joseph II of Bavaria married Maria-Anna Sophia, the granddaughter of the Elector Augustus the Strong of Saxony, who founded the Meissen factory. Having inherited her family's passion for porcelain, the new bride persuaded her husband to open his own factory in an old hunting lodge at Neudeck. The factory opened in the year of the marriage and was at first managed by Franz Ignaz Niedermayer, whose work has not yet been identified, but the manufacture of porcelain did not begin in earnest until 1753, when the ceramist Johann Jakob Ringler arrived from Vienna. In 1761, the factory was moved to a new building near the Elector's palace at Nymphenburg, where it has remained ever since.

Paste and glaze
The best Nymphenburg porcelain belongs to the early period, until c.1770. The hard-paste is white, close-grained and flawless. The equally flawless glaze is usually warm and wet-looking. It is often a little opaque, like tin-glaze, but it can also be translucent. Sometimes it seems slightly smoky or grey, and it occasionally has a greenish-creamy appearance, especially where it has pooled in crevices or at the points where spouts and handles join the main body.

Designs

The most common useful wares made at Nymphenburg are tea and coffee services, plates, tankards, ice-pails or *cachepôts* (for holding a flower pot), and cylindrical food-warmers (usually known as *veilleuses* or *réchauds*).

* Early coffee cups have a simple "U" shape with a slightly out-turned rim. The handle is an "S" scroll with two small shoots about a third of the way up from the lower junction, one projecting away from the cup and the other turned inwards.
* Tea cups are shallow and often have very complex ear-shaped handles with two rudimentary "nodes" projecting towards the cup.
* Sugar bowls are usually "U"-shaped and have small stepped rims and domed covers with terraced ridges or reeding on the edge.
* Tankards are plain and cylindrical with handles shaped like question marks.
* *Veilleuses* are also cylindrical and have vertically ribbed, bell-shaped handles, ridged feet and thick, ring-shaped mouth-rims. Their large, domed covers are surmounted by stalk-shaped knops.
* *Cachepôts* follow the designs of contemporary silver with subtle, rounded shapes, gadrooned feet and pierced, plant-shaped handles.

Nymphenburg teapots made between 1755 and 1765 are particularly characteristic and easily recognized. This example is typical. The shape is always compressed, with sides that straighten or curve outwards at the foot. The handle is a double "C" scroll, with a plain, small scroll below and a large, grooved and finely reeded scroll above. The spout, which is relatively long and terminates above the level of the rim, takes the form of a swan's neck and head and often has what looks like a tube projecting from the beak. The cover is a shallow dome with a neat groove on the rim; the knop is a closed artichoke.

* The coffee pot from the same period has a short "pinched" spout moulded in low relief with Rococo scrolls.

Decoration

The decoration on Nymphenburg wares is usually very skilfully and sensitively painted. The finest and most popular type represents birds in the branches of trees or loose bouquets of flowers, such as those on the plates in the main picture. Other popular decorative themes are:-
* landscapes containing classical ruins and statues in the manner of J. E. Nilson, whose work was copied by many German porcelain and *faïence* factories
* Chinese figures and characters from the *Commedia dell' Arte*
* pastoral scenes in the 17thC style of the Teniers family
* livestock, particularly cattle, in the style of another 17thC Dutch painter, Nicolas Berchem.

All these scenes can be unframed, half-enclosed by Rococo scrolls in a variety of colours, or entirely surrounded by Sèvres-style Rococo scrolls in gold and blue.

In the early 19thC the factory continued to follow Sèvres and imitated the Neo-classical French Empire style.

Palette

The Nymphenburg palette consists of:-
* ochre
* puce
* mushroom-pink
* sky-blue
* greyish, almost olive, green
* yellow
* brownish red
* brown
* gilding.

Marks

Nymphenburg porcelain is almost always marked with an impressed shield derived from the *rautensschild* of Bavaria. The mark, which is sometimes very conspicuous, measures between a quarter and half an inch (0.6-1.2cm) across. Although the shape varies, it is always cross-hatched diagonally.

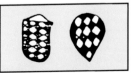

NYMPHENBURG FIGURES

Nymphenburg figures of Harlequin *and* Lalage *from the* Commedia dell'Arte *by Bustelli c.1760; ht 8in/20cm; value code A*

Identification checklist for Nymphenburg figures before 1763

1. Is the porcelain hard-paste?
2. Is it free from imperfections?
3. Is the figure marked with an impressed shield?
4. Does the figure grow from its base?
5. Is the base flat with slight Rococo curves at the edges?
6. Is the lower part of the figure a bit elongated?
7. Is it exceptionally light in weight?
8. If figures are in pairs, are they reacting to each other?
9. Are the folds on the clothes sharply defined?
10. Does the body twist?

Franz Anton Bustelli (1722-1763)

The finest of all the Nymphenburg products are the figures modelled by the mysterious Franz Anton Bustelli, who worked at Neudeck and Nymphenburg from 1754 until his death in 1763. Nothing is known about him before he came to Nymphenburg, other than that he was born in Switzerland in 1722, but as a modeller for porcelain, he was second only to J. J. Kändler at Meissen. The 150 figures which he modelled during his eight and a half years at Nymphenburg are indisputable evidence of genius.

Style

Where Kändler was the master of the Baroque, modelling luxuriously on a broad plane, Bustelli was the master of the Rococo, modelling with graceful economy within the limitations of his material. Bustelli's figures are detached and ethereal; they have none of the slightly cruel realism which characterizes the work of the German modellers. The lower parts of Bustelli's models are a little elongated, in the traditional Bavarian style, but the expressive faces and the contrast between flowing lines and busy surfaces have much in common with the work of the Viennese sculptor Ignaz Gunther, which has led some experts to suggest that Bustelli must have studied with him. Bustelli often modelled his figures as interacting pairs. For example, the *Commedia dell'Arte* figures *opposite*, were made to be displayed together, with *Harlequin* holding up the monkey dressed as a child and *Lalage* reaching out to feed it.

Subjects

Apart from allegorical figures and characters from the *Commedia dell'Arte*, Bustelli's most important subjects were:- Chinese characters and scenes; Turks and Moors; ladies and gentlemen; merchants and street vendors; shepherds and shepherdesses; religious subjects and dogs and cats.

The essential elements in Bustelli's unique style are obvious even in the simplest figures, such as this *Leda* from the *Commedia dell'Arte*. The contrast between the shapes is accentuated by the broad expanse of pastel yellow on the dress and the bold brocaded bodice. The tilt of the head, the twist of the body and the movement in the hand are all typical of Bustelli's modelling. Above all, no other modeller could define the folds of a dress so sharply or reveal the limbs beneath it with so much sensuous subtlety.

Bustelli's preoccupation with contrasts expressed itself as much in his choice of subjects as in his shapes and colours. One famous allegorical series of figures, made between 1755 and 58, depicts the omnipotent classical gods as frail and harmless human babies playing with the symbols of their power. Around 1760 four of these *putti* gods were adapted to make a new series, entitled *The Four Seasons*, which included this representation of *Summer*.

Many of Bustelli's figures, such as this fishmonger, have been left in the white. Without the colour, his mastery of movement becomes even more apparent.

Bases

Unlike the figures of other modellers, which look as though they have been attached to their bases, Bustelli's figures seem to grow out of them. The earliest stand on flat bases with slight, asymmetrical Rococo curves at the edges. However, some of the later figures, particularly the groups, have mound-shaped bases surrounded by Rococo decorations with scrolls rising out of them to form part of the composition.

Dominikus Jakob Auliczek

After Bustelli's death his successor, Dominikus Jakob Auliczek, added a few more animal figures to the repertoire, including several brutal hunting groups depicting hounds attacking their prey.

FÜRSTENBERG WARES

A Fürstenberg oval dish
1765-70; lgth 12-14in/30.5-35.5cm; value code E.

Identification checklist for Fürstenberg wares
1. Is the porcelain hard-paste?
2. Is the glaze off-white and glittery?
3. Is the palette dominated by dark browns and greens?
4. Is the piece decorated in monochrome purple or green?
5. Does it have elaborate moulding?
6. Are the handles on cups and pots formed by an exaggerated "C"-scroll on a small inverted crescent, or are they ear-shaped?
7. Is the rim of the piece decorated with flimsy scrollwork and a spider's web motif?
8. If the piece is a pot, does it have galleried rims on the cover, below the neck and around the base?
9. Is the piece decorated with moulded ribbonwork?

Fürstenberg (1753-c.1800)
The Duke of Brunswick established a factory at Fürstenberg in 1747, but it did not begin to manufacture porcelain until 1753, when the management was entrusted to Johann Benckgraff, until then the manager of the factory at Höchst. Benckgraff brought with him two of Höchst's best artists, the painter Johann Zeschinger and the modeller Simon Feilner, and their influence is clearly evident in many of the factory's early products.

Paste and glaze
The Fürstenberg hard-paste is close-grained and white, and looks very similar to the body of Meissen or Berlin. The glaze is off-white and glittery.

Moulding
Elaborate moulded scrollwork was used on early wares to disguise flaws in the paste. As on the dish *above*, it was often highlighted with brassy gilding.

Decoration
Early themes such as flowers and landscapes are typical of the German Rococo. Many decorations are painted *en camaïeu* (in a single colour – usually purple or green) and are either enclosed in contrasting scrolls or else float unframed in the middle of the plate or vessel. Landscapes are similar to those from Ludwigsburg, although they are often on a slightly larger scale in relation to the size of the vessel. Most are based on engravings by the Flemish artists Waterloo and Weirotter.

Palette
The palette is dominated by browns and greens. The main colours are:
* dark, reddish brown
* tan
* iron-red
* chrome yellow
* dirty turquoise
* puce
* lilac
* dark green
* yellowish green
* grey green
* greyish blue
* gilding (used copiously).

Meissen in the 1720s. However, they could not be mistaken for Meissen wares as the Fürstenberg palette is very different.
* The spider's web motif and flimsy scrollwork on the rim are characteristic of the Fürstenberg factory.

Although the Rococo handles might be Sèvres, the heavy shape of this *potpourri* vase, made around 1770, is uniquely Fürstenberg.
* The piece is also decorated in one of the factory's most easily identified themes – meticulous *vignettes* of poultry and other birds perched on branches or fences, painted by C. G. Albert.

The pear-shaped coffee pot is common to most German factories, but the Fürstenberg version, with its heavy belly, thick neck and exaggerated "C"-scroll handle, is less elegant than the others. This example, made around 1755, is painted in *camaïeu purpurin* (monochrome purple) in the manner of Watteau.

Much of Fürstenberg's decoration was behind the times. This cup and saucer, made in the late 1760s, are painted with Chinoiserie scenes which were fashionable at

The shapes of the pieces in this service, which was made between 1780 and 1785, indicate the transition between the Rococo and the Neo-classical at Fürstenberg. The restraint is Neo-classical, but the ear-shaped handles and the spouts, although now much heavier, are still essentially Rococo.
* Fürstenberg produced a large number of Neo-classical wares painted with monochrome or slightly drab panels.

FÜRSTENBERG FIGURES

A Fürstenberg "inkstandish", modelled by Heinrich Wegener
1765; ht 14 ¾ in/37.5cm; value code B/C

Identification checklist for Fürstenberg figures
1. Is the porcelain hard-paste?
2. Does it contain little black flecks?
3. Are figures set on simple pad or mound bases?
4. Are the groups set on elaborate scroll bases?
5. Are the figures rather stiff with pursed lips and severe expressions?
6. Are the subjects stockily built?
7. Is the modelling very crisp?
8. If the figure is a miner, has it been left in the white?
9. Is the figure marked with a script capital "F"?

Figures

The Fürstenberg factory made a number of classical figures based on bronzes or ivories, which may account for the fine, crisp modelling. Others were based on models from other factories, such as Berlin, Höchst and particularly Meissen. However, the Fürstenberg figures have a twisting sense of power, and they are more compact than most northern European figures. Like the figures on the inkwell, copied from a Berlin original, they also have more highly coloured skin.

Subjects

The most usual subjects are:
* gentlemen (known as "gallants") and their companions
* *Commedia dell'Arte* characters
* artisans, particularly miners
* classical gods
* contemporary costumes; the finest were modelled by Simon Feilner. His early figures were elongated and a little stiff, but have the characteristic Fürstenberg pursed lips and disapproving expression. They were set on plain, Meissen-like pad bases decorated with flowers.

This candlestick group is almost identical to a group that Feilner made at Höchst, and once again it has the elongation and stiffness that are so typical of his early work. However, in addition to the mark, there are several features which identify the piece as Fürstenberg:
* the material is flawed and contains little black flecks
* as the paste is more plastic than the Höchst paste, there is a large cross-shaped support beneath the base to stop it collapsing in the firing.

These figures were made by Desoches and Hendler, two of the leading modellers at Fürstenberg in the 1770s. Desoches' figure of *Summer* on the *left* is typical of the transition from Rococo to Neo-classicism. The striped and flowered skirt is entirely Neo-classical, but the scrolls on the base are Rococo. Desoches was a Frenchman, and not surprisingly, his figures are much more French-looking than other Fürstenberg figures. For example, they have pretty faces and their features are more even. Nevertheless, the slightly chopped base identifies the figure as Fürstenberg.

The group of *Venus and Cupid*, *right*, is by Hendler and is the last that he made at the factory. The circular base, moulded with a Greek meander pattern, is typical of the Neo-classical figures produced by many other factories. Like most of Hendler's figures, the bodies are stiff and not anatomically correct, but like those made by Desoches, they have sweeter features and lack the disapproving expression of other Fürstenberg figures.

Feilner's miners were among his finest figures. Kändler also made a series of miners at Meissen, but Feilner's are easily distinguished from the more comfortable-looking Meissen versions:
* the bodies are well-muscled
* the strong, distinctive faces have high cheekbones, pointed noses and hooded eyes
* the proportions are realistic and the crisp folds on the clothes look as though they have been carved rather than modelled
* the fingers are very detailed
* most of Feilner's figures were so good that they were left in the white – Kändler's were invariably coloured.

Copies
The Fürstenberg factory carried on into the 19thC, when the original 18thC moulds were used to produce clumsily decorated copies of the original figures.

Marks
The Fürstenberg mark is one of the simplest: a script capital "F" in underglaze blue. However, although some versions are very straightforward, others are very hastily written and barely recognizable.
* Neo-classical figures, particularly biscuit busts of ancient poets and philosophers, were sometimes impressed with a horse from the arms of Brunswick.

81

FULDA

*Part of a Fulda tea and coffee service
c.1765; value code C*

Identification checklist for Fulda porcelain
1. Is the paste almost flawless?
2. Is the glaze warm and creamy?
3. If the piece is a ware, is it decorated with a landscape *vignette* with trailing foliage and roots?
4. Is the decoration framed or partially framed by puce and russet brown feathered scrolls?
5. Is the foreground predominantly deep brown?
6. Are the handles on vessels formed in a treble scroll?
7. Are painted landscapes reminiscent of Meissen?
8. Is the modelling of figures very detailed but a little stiff?
9. Does the figure have a doll-like face with rosy cheeks, a tiny nose and pinpoint eyes?
10. Do any leaves and flowers on the base of figures stand proud?
11. Has the base been edged in shallow, puce Rococo scrolls which look like an afterthought?
12. Is the mark right? (see *opposite*)

Fulda (1764-90)

In 1764, Johann Philipp Schick, who had been running a *faïence* factory at Fulda for some time, persuaded the prince bishop, Heinrich von Bibra, to open a porcelain factory. Schick, who knew little about porcelain, hired Nikolaus Paul, an arcanist who had worked at the Weesp factory in Holland. Paul stayed for only a year, but by the time he left Fulda was making an almost perfect paste with a warm, creamy glaze, easily comparable to the products of Nymphenburg or Meissen. And yet, despite its high quality wares, the factory only lasted until 1790.

Wares

All the Fulda products are made with great care and skill, but, like the artists at so many other German factories, the Fulda painters seem to have been unable to break away from the Meissen tradition. Their landscapes, figures and scattered sprays of *deutsche Blumen* are invariably derivative. Nevertheless, Fulda wares do have distinguishing features:

* On early wares (see main picture) the landscapes are *vignettes* with foliage and roots hanging down from the scene like seaweed. These dangling plants can also be found on many Fürstenberg wares, but on Fulda wares, like the rest of the foreground, they are dominated by a deep autumnal brown.
* On later wares, landscape and figure subjects are partially or completely enclosed within a frame of strange, elaborately feathered Rococo scrolls painted in puce and russet.
* Some landscapes are painted *en camaïeu* (in monochrome brown or black).
* The handles on many vessels are formed in a treble scroll.
* The pineapple knops are much bolder than on most other wares.
* After about 1775, the factory concentrated on the production of wares and turned to the Neo-classical style. Favourite themes on these later wares were medallion heads and portraits framed by wreaths of leaves or husks.

Palette

The Fulda palette consists mostly of:
* greyish blue
* green
* egg-yolk yellow
* orange
* rust-brown
* iron-red
* puce
* black
* gilding.

Figures

The Fulda factory is justly famous for its figures. Among the finest are the characters from the *Commedia dell' Arte*, modelled by Wenzel Neu, and the series of the Fulda court orchestra and the *Cries of Paris*, modelled by G. L. Bartoleme, who came from the Ansbach factory in 1770, and whose work has a lot in common with that of the famous Johann Friedrich Lück of Frankenthal.

This delicate group, c.1780, of a gentlemen flirting with a lady while out shooting has many characteristic Fulda features:
* The modelling, although a little stiff, is also meticulous and the use of colour unusually sensitive.
* The calm, untroubled faces are doll-like with chubby, rosy cheeks, tiny noses and pinpoint eyes.
* The brittle, curving, lifelike leaves and flowers stand up proud from the base (a feature peculiar to Fulda figures).

These two figures show Fulda bases of the later period. The lady on the *left* stands on a simple base washed in green and brown, but the sultana on the *right* stands on a mound base embellished with shallow Rococo scrolls By this time other factories were making simple Neo-classical architectural bases.

Marks

Between 1764 and 1780, the mark was a cross in underglaze blue. From 1781 to 1788, the mark was a crown over a double, upper case script "F" (the "Heinrich mark"). During the last year of the factory's life, the "Fs" were interlaced (the "Adalbert mark", named after Heinrich's successor).

MINOR THURINGIAN FACTORIES

A pair of Limbach figures representing Europe and Asia
c.1775; ht 7 ³/₄ in/20cm; value code E.

Identification checklist for the porcelain of the minor
Thuringian factories
1. Is the porcelain hard-paste?
2. Is it on the whole a bit grey?
3. Is the piece trying to pass itself off as Meissen or,
alternatively, is it an obvious copy of some other factory,
such as Wedgwood?
4. If a figure, does it have naïve, doll-like features?
5. Is the modelling of the figure crude?

The Thuringian factories
The nine small factories in the
Saxon province of Thuringia were
established in the third quarter of
the 18thC, at a time when the
most famous German factories
had reached their prime or even
passed it. Like all the great
German factories, the most
important in Thuringia, Closter-
Veilsdorf (see pp. 86-87), was
founded by a prince, but the other
factories were founded by
merchants and amateur chemists,
whose down-to-earth business

instincts kept them going long
after many of the more creative
establishments had been forced to
close.
   Although the only Thuringian
pieces with any artistic merit were
made during the last quarter of the
18thC, some of the factories
survived well into the 19th and
even the 20thC, producing
unaffected figures of peasants,
numerous copies of figures from
other German factories and
simple, highly commercial but
usually second-rate tableware.

Gotha
The oldest Thuringian factory, Gotha, may have been established as early as 1757, but it did not begin to flourish until ten years later.

Of all Thuringian porcelain, that made by Gotha is the most carefully decorated. The paste is light and transparent, and the glaze is very soft and creamy. The best pieces are:
* wares decorated with polychrome flowers or pastoral scenes
* presentation pieces, such as fine silhouetted cups
* mythological figures and busts made in an unglazed, marble-like, white porcelain.

Volkstedt
The factory at Volkstedt was founded in 1760 by a clergyman with an interest in natural sciences. It owed its survival to the patronage of the princes of Schwarzburg-Rudolstadt, who eventually became proprietors. The early hard-paste porcelain is heavy and grey and has an unclear glaze. Painters used scattered flowers to hide the many bubbles and fire-cracks. Later porcelain, although better, is still flawed, but on many wares the flaws are camouflaged by the Rococo modelling.
* Many wares are crude copies of Meissen (see p. 48-49).

Volkstedt's hard-paste was well suited to modelling. As a result, some of its finest early products are bright and ingeniously animated rural figures, like this pair collecting a bird's nest.

Wallendorf
Wallendorf was established in 1764 by a group which included the cousins Johann Gottfried Greiner and Gotthelf Greiner. The porcelain they made is light and transparent, although the glaze is thick and yellowish. The figure modelling is clumsy. Specialities are pipe-bowls and little cups with no handles.

Gera
Established in 1779, Gera was taken over after initial financial difficulties by Johann Georg Wilhelm and Johann Andreas, the sons of Johann Gottfried Greiner. Most products are Neo-classical. The porcelain is generally of poor quality although this is masked by decoration.

One of the most characteristic decorations is a brown surface painted to represent wood.

Limbach
Second in importance to Closter-Veilsdorf, Limbach was founded in 1772 by Gotthelf Greiner, who had just retired from Wallendorf. The early porcelain is slightly yellow, but the later glaze has a lighter, more delicate quality.
* The most successful products are stiff, charmingly naïve figures. Most of them represent peasants and citizens and imaginary royalty in unlikely, theatrical robes.
* The best of the early wares are superficial copies of Meissen, many marked deceptively with a pair of crossed Ls and a star. But in 1787, under pressure from Meissen, the mark was changed to a trefoil.

Ilmenau
Founded in 1777, Ilmenau was leased by Gotthelf Greiner between 1782 and 92, when he assigned it to the managership of Volkstedt.
* According to the poet Goethe, who decorated some wares himself, the paste was of very poor quality.
* The factory made some blue and white imitations of Wedgwood.

Grossbreitenbach
Established in the late 1770s, Grossbreitenbach was sold in 1782 to Gotthelf Greiner, who made it a branch of the Limbach factory.

Rauenstein
Rauenstein was established in 1783 by three Greiners who were probably not related to Johann Gottfried and Gotthelf.
* Most products were copies.

CLOSTER-VEILSDORF

*A Closter-Veilsdorf tea and coffee service,
c.1770; value code D*

Identification checklist for Closter-Veilsdorf porcelain
1. Is the porcelain hard-paste?
2. Is the paste smooth, milk-white and almost flawless (see *facing page*)?
3. On pieces from tea and coffee sets, is the handle complex (See *facing page*.)?
4. Is any moulding confined to the bottom half of the vessel?
5. Is the moulding basketweave, shells or a flowery diaper?
6. On wares, is the painting detailed and realistic?
7. Is the landscape framed in drapery?
8. If the piece is a figure, is it small?
9. Does the figure stand on a simple mound or one that is lightly carved with scrolls?
10. Is the face quite highly coloured?
11. Is there a lack of detail in the modelling?
12. Is the mark right (see *facing page*)?

Closter-Veilsdorf
The most important of the Thuringian factories founded in the third quarter of the 18thC was Closter-Veilsdorf. Established in 1760 by Prince Friedrich Wilhelm Eugen von Hildburghausen, the factory was sold off two years after his death, in 1795, to the five sons of Gotthelf Greiner (see pp.84-5).

Early hard-paste
Closter-Veilsdorf's early products are made of a very smooth, milk-white and almost unblemished porcelain. Only occasionally do a few of the pieces have a tiny iron-spot flaw about the size of a pin head. However, after 1770, both

paste and glaze became slightly grey, even though the paste was still very close-grained.

Palette
The dominant colours in the Closter-Veilsdorf palette are:-
* pale puce
* iron-red
* yellow
* greyish blue
* green
* grey.

Note
Turquoise, although popular at other factories, especially in the Rococo period, was apparently never used at Closter-Veilsdorf.

Wares

Before about 1780 the wares made at Closter-Veilsdorf followed the general Rococo style adopted by most of the German and Austrian factories. Many vessels from this period have moulded borders of shells or basketweave in the manner of Meissen around the bottom half. Others have a more exuberant confection of scrollwork and flowery diaper. In either case, the edges are often heightened in puce.

Handles

The handles of cups and hollow vessels are often very complex, and some, particularly on teapots and coffee pots, are decidedly eccentric. Some teapots and coffee pots have as many as five alternate "C" scrolls, which creates a rather knobbly Gothic effect. Another common type is similar to the wishbone shape of Zürich (see pp.90-1), and is composed of "S" and "C" scrolls modelled with small vestigial stems projecting from opposite sides.

The finest Closter-Veilsdorf figures are the *Commedia dell'Arte* characters modelled by Wenzel Neu like that shown *above*. A Bohemian by birth, Neu began his career at the Fulda factory in 1742. After a brief stay at the Thuringian factory of Volkstedt, he came to Closter-Veilsdorf in 1762 and remained until 1767, when he returned to Fulda. The other most popular subjects for modelling at Closter-Veilsdorf were classical and Oriental figures. The factory's figures are usually small (not more than 7in/17.5cm). They have little definition – for example, the fingers are not separate – and the faces, which are quite highly coloured, lack character. However, the final result is usually charming. The bases for the figures are simple mounds sometimes lightly carved with scrolls.

Decoration

The decorative themes on wares from Closter-Veilsdorf are conventional and include:
* figure subjects in the style of Teniers or Watteau
* cherubs in the manner of Boucher
* landscapes framed in drapery
* portrait medallions
* birds
* flowers
* Chinoiseries.
Several Closter-Veilsdorf designs were based on drawings by Prince Friedrich Wilhelm. Although little is known about the decorators, it is evident that some of them were very skilful, particularly as painters of birds, fruit and flowers. Despite the awkward Rococo shapes, the painters managed to decorate the wares with sensitivity and with a degree of realism that was not often achieved at other factories.

Marks

The usual factory mark, rendered in underglaze blue, is composed of the letters C and V, either combined in a monogram or separate.
* On some early pieces the letters are accompanied by the shield of Saxony.
* Another underglaze blue mark is the simple three-petalled flower-head, which is also found on the products of two other Thuringian factories Limbach and Groszbreitenbach.

BERLIN

A Berlin Neo-classical fruit bowl and stand
c.1795-1800; dia. 9½in/24cm; value code D/E

Identification checklist for Berlin porcelain
1. Is the porcelain hard-paste?
2. Is it slightly greyish-white with a creamy, opaque glaze?
3. Is the appearance glassy and bluish?
4. Does any enamel decoration display patches of flaking?
5. Is the piece moulded in any way?
6. Does it have rustic handles?
7. If a figure, is it set on a square, slab base?
8. Do the figure's feet project?
9. Are the marks right? (see *opposite*)

Berlin (1752-present)
The first Berlin factory, founded in 1752 by Wilhelm Kaspar Wegely, closed in 1757. However, the second, founded in 1761 by Johann Ernst Gotzkowsky, survived to become one of the most influential of the 20thC.

Wegely paste and glaze
The early paste is of fine white porcelain, not unlike Meissen – in fact both factories obtained most of their material from the same source.
* The glaze on this early material is thin and colourless and tends to be opaque.

Wegely wares
Wegely produced decorative wares, such as vases, often liberally encrusted with flowers and human masks and with figures on the lid. Tea and coffee wares often have moulded Oriental flowers, although some were plain-surfaced.

Wegely decoration
Decorations tended to follow the Meissen style, with landscapes, Watteauesque figures and semi-botanical subjects. However, the glaze did not accept enamelling well, and in many cases small areas have flaked.

The pear-shaped form and the spout of this coffee pot, made c.1755, are very similar to Meissen, although the crabstock handle and trailing Oriental foliage are distinctly Wegely.

Wegely figures

Wegely produced a range of figures, either copied from Meissen, such as cupids and *Commedia dell'Arte* characters, or created from printed sources, such as huntsmen and artisans. He also made small, classical figures of the seasons on high, square pedestals. Although many examples are left in the white, some are painted with solid washes in which puce, iron-red and black predominate.

Gotzkowsky's paste and glaze

The paste remained virtually the same at Gotzkowsky's factory until about 1770, when new materials were employed. These produced a colder looking paste with a greyish tone to it.
* The glaze was also colder than before and had a more bluish tone.

Gotzkowsky's wares

Some of the finest Berlin porcelains were made with this new clay, between 1770 and 86, when the factory transformed Meissen and Sèvres models into a delicate, late Rococo style of its own, employing shallow moulded decoration with a scaled pattern.

This figure of a Tyrolean pedlar was modelled by Wilhelm Meyer in 1769. It is characteristically painted in black, pale salmon pink and puce and has the typical small, square base.

This pair of soup plates, made for Frederick the Great in 1768, depict characteristically delicate flowers.
* The borders are decorated in shallow, moulded relief (or *reliefzierat*) in a pleated-looking configuration (unique to Berlin) with feather-edged scrolls.
* The moulded rim is detailed with typically hesitant Berlin gilding.

Gotzkowsky's figures

The most famous series of figures made during Gotzkowsky's ownership was *The Cries of Berlin*, modelled by Friedrich and Wilhelm Meyer. The brothers also made a number of classical figures, usually with allegorical themes. These figures are often elongated and have relatively small heads.
* Apart from the early Rococo bases, most of Gotzkowsky's figures are mounted on simple, square slabs.

This is a fine Neo-classical landscape plate signed by the factory's leading painter, Lefaure, and dated 1817. In common with Vienna, Paris and Derby, Berlin used the porcelain as a vehicle for miniature painting. Entire plates were covered with similar enamelling and gilding, often making it impossible to identify the factory by its style or its paste.

Marks

Wegely's mark is an underglaze or an impressed "W", sometimes accompanied by fractional numbers representing the type of paste and series numbers of the moulds.

Gotzkowsky's marks included a "G", a sceptre taken from the arms of Brandenburg, or the Hapsburg eagle over the initials "KPM" – when this is red, it represents 1823-32; blue and red were used 1832-44, and blue only from 1844 onwards. From 1832, an orb over the initials "KPM" was also used.

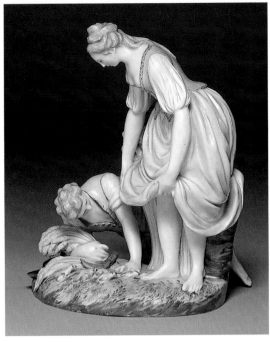

A Zürich allegorical group of lovers, representing Summer
c.1770; ht 6¼in/16cm; value code D/E

Identification checklist for 18thC Zürich porcelain
1. Is the glaze greyish or smoky-cream?
2. If the piece is a figure, is it slightly stiffly moulded?
3. Is the figure painted in broad washes and rather pale pastel colours?
4. Is the base of the figure moulded as simple rockwork or a mossy mound?
5. If the piece is a ware, is it decorated with a particularly fine landscape vignette?
6. Are the leaves on the trees in the landscape a greyish green and finely detailed in black or brown?
7. If the piece is a teapot or a jug, does it have an unusually complex scrolled handle? (see *opposite*)
8. Is it marked with a "Z" in underglaze blue?

Zürich (1763-1897)
The most important porcelain factory in Switzerland was founded at Scoren near Zurich in 1763. One of the founders was the pastoral poet and landscape painter Salomon Gessner. The first director was A. Spengler, whose son Jean-Jacques worked there as a modeller before going on to become the leading modeller at Derby in England.

Paste and glaze

At first the factory made a soft-paste, which is now very rare, but hard-paste was introduced around 1765, using kaolin from Lorraine. The hard-paste is composed of a greyish and granular body, which has sometimes burned to a reddish or brownish colour in the firing.
* The quite glassy glaze has a greyish or smoky cream colour, not unlike the glaze of Ludwigsburg. On a few pieces the glaze has become rough and crumbly.

Wares

Tea and coffee wares from Zurich follow the usual German Rococo and Neo-classical patterns. Some are ribbed and decorated in puce with *indianische Blumen*, like the late 18thC wares from Copenhagen and the minor Thuringian factories.
* Cups are tall, with simple loop or wishbone-shaped handles.
* Teapots are usually bullet-shaped with flush lids surmounted by bud knops. The complex handles have two "S" scrolls separated by a small "C" scroll.

Landscapes

Under the influence of Salomon Gessner, who designed and painted the decoration on many of the wares himself, the most common themes are inevitably landscapes and pastoral scenes, usually painted as vignettes. The quality of the landscapes at Zürich in the 1760s and 70s was consistently high. Some of the finest were painted by Heinrich Thomann and Heinrich Fuseli.

The soft landscape vignette by Heinrich Thomann on this beautiful hot-milk jug is typical of the decoration on Zürich wares from the 1770s. In common with the country scenes on so many 18thC German wares, the painting

is based on the work of a 17thC artist from the Low Countries, in this case Anton Waterloo, whose engravings were particularly popular among porcelain painters.
* The jug also has the characteristic Zürich handle.

Other themes

The other decorative themes are:-
* birds
* Meissen-style flowers
* Oriental flowers
* blue and white.

Palette

The dominant early colours are:-
* soft russet
* sky blue
* puce
* greyish yellow
* manganese purple.
In the 1780s two brighter colours were added:-
* a stronger russet
* lemon-yellow.

Figures

Zürich made very attractive but static figures. The best were modelled by J. V. Sonnenschein, who came from Ludwigsburg in the late 1770s, and their broad washes and pale colours are reminiscent of the Ludwigsburg style.

The slightly stiff modelling of Zürich figures is particularly apparent in these miniatures of a trinket seller and a pattern seller. The little figures (less than 4in/10.16cm) were made c.1773 and come from a series which was widely collected at the time.

Mark

The mark of the Zürich factory is a "Z" in underglaze blue with a horizontal line through its mid-point. The mark is sometimes accompanied by a number of dots. The factory ceased production towards the end of the 19thC.

ST CLOUD

A moulded St Cloud strainer cup with underglaze blue decoration
1700-25; ht 3-4in/7.6-10cm; value code E/F

Identification checklist for St Cloud porcelain
1. Is the porcelain soft-paste?
2. Is the glaze quite glassy?
3. Are there black flecks in the surface of the piece?
4. If it is polychrome, is it decorated in the Kakiemon style?
5. Are any handles very thick?
6. Does the underglaze blue decoration resemble miniature wrought-ironwork?

St Cloud (1664-1766)
The earliest recorded attempt to manufacture porcelain in France was in 1664, when Claude and François Reverend were granted the right to set up a factory at St Cloud between Paris and Versailles. However, there are no extant examples which can be ascribed to a date before the 1690s. Martin Lister, an English doctor, visited the factory in 1698 and wrote that the director, François de Morin, had only recently perfected his porcelain after experimenting for 25 years. Lister said he could discern no difference between St Cloud porcelain and Chinese porcelain, except that he felt St Cloud's decoration was more accomplished than the Oriental.

Wares
The variety of vessels and decorative wares produced by St Cloud include:
* circular soup tureens and covers
* teapots with dragon or bird's neck handles and spouts
* figure- or bird-shaped jugs
* Chinoiserie *potpourri* encrusted with flowers and supported on rockwork bases
* "three-limbed" spice boxes
* flower-encrusted baskets
* handles for canes and knives
* salts in "waisted" capstan or chamfered rectangular shapes
* conical candlesticks
* cylindrical pots
* cups and saucers, butter dishes, jam pots and cruet stands
* snuff boxes
* ice pails.

The curling handles on pots, jugs and cups are always thick and are either grooved or slab-sided.
* On larger vessels, such as tureens, the handles are modelled in the form of monstrous, gaping animal masks.

Decoration
On early pieces the underglaze blue decoration often includes miniature wrought-ironwork in the style of the late French Baroque.
* From c.1730 onwards, polychrome enamelling follows the fashion for Kakiemon, but it is primitive and stiff and the colours are nothing like the Japanese palette.
* Due to the sumptuary laws (see p. 100) there is little gilding.

Palette
The dominant colours are:
* dirty, egg-yolk yellow
* yellowish green
* turquoise
* sky blue
* blood red
* black.

Paste and glaze
St Cloud soft-paste uses a fine, greyish-white paste, often with tiny black flecks. The glaze is creamy white with hints of olive green where it has pooled. It is less shiny than the Mennecy glaze and gives a warm satin-like sheen.

This *bonbonnière*, modelled as a shepherd, is typical of the small pieces made at St Cloud in the mid-18thC. Less than 3in (7.5cm) tall, it is decorated throughout with delicate flowers in the Kakiemon style and is, typically, mounted on silver. The French control marks on the silver help to date these pieces.
* Figures made by St Cloud in the earlier 18thC (mainly Chinoiserie) are usually more finely detailed than the shepherd. Most are in white, with nothing to distract from their crisp modelling.

A feature of many early St Cloud wares is moulding based on Chinese motifs. However, the flowers tend to be more realistic than the stylized Chinese versions, with sharper, more delicate detailing than on the heavily glazed Chinese originals. Other mouldings include wading birds and overlapping leaves, like the surface of an artichoke.

Elaborate *potpourri* vases such as this became a speciality of the factory in the middle of the 18thC. They are usually in the white, almost always encrusted with flowers and often set on moulded rockwork bases.

Marks
The most common St Cloud mark is an incised "St C" over a "T", standing for the Trou family, which acquired the factory by marriage at the end of the 17thC.
* Another quite common mark is a painted sun with a face on it.

CHANTILLY

A Chantilly figure of a Chinaman
c.1730-40; ht 8in/20.5cm; value code C

Identification checklist for Chantilly porcelain before c.1750

1. Is the piece soft-paste?
2. Is the glaze creamy and opaque?
3. If the piece is a figure, does it have Chinoiserie decoration?
4. Is the modelling of any figures indistinct and lacking in detail, particularly on the face and hands?
5. If enamelled, do the colours reflect the typical Kakiemon palette (see facing page), and are they painstakingly outlined in black?
6. If not enamelled, does the piece have a white body painted in underglaze blue or in conventional Rococo colours dominated by puce and brown?
7. Does the decoration have a stiff linear quality, and show signs of detailed brushwork?
8. Is the piece marked?
9. Is it fairly small (see Note below)?

Identification point
Like Chantilly, Meissen outlined their colours in black. However, their porcelain has a cold, glassy translucent glaze, whereas that of Chantilly is distinctively creamy and opaque – the result of adding tin to conceal imperfections.

Note
Most wares are under 10in (25.4cm) tall, probably because above that size soft-paste pieces tended to sag or collapse in the kiln. On larger items, look out for cracks, splits or tears, sometimes obscured by the decoration.

Kakiemon-style wares

Many items were close copies of Kakiemon wares, both in form and in decoration. It is probable that such pieces were copied directly from specimens in the personal collection of the Prince de Condé (see *right*). The seated figure, *opposite*, is typical of Chantilly Kakiemon in a number of ways:

* The patterns have a flat, linear appearance, common to many Kakiemon-type wares, as the enamels tended to sink into the glaze. However, the use of black outlining helps to distinguish Chantilly wares both from the more painterly style of true Japanese enamelling and from the Kakiemon wares made by other French porcelain factories during the early 18thC, such as St Cloud and Mennecy.
* The brushwork is highly detailed, especially on the robes, which are decorated with scattered flowers.
* The distinct lack of detailed modelling, particularly in the face and on the hands, is typical of the factory's early soft-paste figures. Like all European attempts at the Oriental, the facial features are somewhat unconvincing.
* The form, which is linear and almost triangular, is weighted at the base to support the figure.

Marks

All wares carry the Chantilly mark of a small hunting horn. This was red until c.1750 and thereafter in a less distinct underglaze blue, or occasionally in other colours, especially red or manganese. A letter sometimes appears under the horn. This may represent the initial letter of the name of the factory's proprietor during the period when the piece was made.

Copies

Beware of imitations of Chantilly by the Paris firm of Samson. These were not originally intended to deceive, but quite often their mark – a pair of tiny entwined "S"s – has been removed. If in doubt, examine the glaze: Samson wares invariably employ a glassy hard-paste porcelain which is very different from the less lustrous soft-paste used by Chantilly.

Chantilly (c.1725-1800)

The factory was established c.1725 under the patronage of the Prince de Condé, an avid collector of Kakiemon, and produced a wide range of useful and decorative wares which typically included:

* figures; almost all Orientals, some shown reclining beside large baluster *potpourri* jars
* bough pots
* jardinières or cachepots
* teapots
* beakers
* small ecuelles or sauce tureens
* plates
* hot water jugs
* coffee pots.

The wavy interrupted outline of this hexafoil Chantilly sweetmeat or oyster stand, c.1735, is typical of the softer profile of the 1730s, which 20 or so years later was to give way to the sinuous curves of the Rococo. It is decorated in the typical Kakiemon colours of iron-red, turquoise, blue, yellow and dark manganese. The emphasis on flower-based motifs is characteristically Japanese. The use of amorphous rockwork in the decoration was popular with all the early French soft-paste factories. Zones of trellis, such as those flanking the flowers of this piece, appear on much European porcelain between c.1775 and c.1750.

Mid-late 18thC wares

Wares made before c.1750 are the most collectable. After this date the Kakiemon style gave way to the sprays of *deutsche Blumen* – in vogue at many French factories as well as at Meissen. The Chantilly interpretation was much looser than the rather academic treatment at the German factory. By the 1760s, the flamboyant Rococo wares of Sèvres had become a major source of inspiration, although Chantilly was forbidden by the royal monopoly to employ gilding. The factory was in decline by c.1780 and closed in 1800.

MENNECY

A Mennecy Chinese figure
c.1735-40; ht 6½in/16.5cm; value code C

Identification checklist for Mennecy porcelain
1. Is the porcelain soft-paste?
2. Is the glaze creamy, glassy and translucent?
3. Is the piece quite small?
4. If the piece is a figure, does it have a pyramid shape?
5. Does the figure have any splits or tears?
6. Is it leaning back and looking upwards?
7. Is it thickly constructed?
8. Are the colours on the figure loose and washed out?
9. If the piece is a small vessel, is it rimmed in puce?
10. If the piece is a cup, is it shaped like a bell or a bucket?

Mennecy (1734-1806)
In 1734 the *faïencier* François Barbin opened a soft-paste factory in Paris, under the patronage of the Duc de Villeroy. Twelve years later, after King Louis XIV had ordered him to stop imitating Vincennes, Barbin moved from the relative safety of the village of Mennecy on the Duke's estates outside the city. When Barbin died in 1766, the factory was bought jointly by the sculptor Joseph Jullien and the painter Charles-Symphorien Jacques, and in 1773 it was moved again, this time to Bourg-la-Reine. In 1780 the factory gave up making porcelain, and from then until its closure in 1806 it made only creamware in the manner of Wedgwood.

Soft-paste
Mennecy manufactured a mellow, ivory-coloured soft-paste porcelain.

The glaze is creamy white, glassy and translucent.

Style
Almost all the figures and wares made by Mennecy are small, probably because of the plasticity of the clay. In its early years the factory imitated not only Vincennes but also St Cloud, Chantilly and even Meissen, but its sensitive interpretation of well-established themes evolved eventually into a style of its own.

Figures
The comparatively rare Mennecy figures are mostly Oriental characters, children at play, rustic groups and naked *putti*. They have fairly heavy pyramid-like shapes – a necessity with soft-paste – and like almost all heavily-potted soft-paste pieces, they often have splits or tears. Nevertheless they are among the most charming and animated figures made in France. Their heads tilt back and gaze upwards (see main picture) and their features are heavily detailed.
* Like all contemporary French factories, Mennecy decorated its early figures in the Kakiemon palette, but the loose, washed-out colours have none of the disciplined precision of Chantilly or the density of St Cloud.
* The invariably heavy, stepped rockwork bases are sometimes pierced and sometimes decorated with applied flowers and moss.

Decorative wares
Decorative wares include baluster vases which are very thickly-potted and tend to fracture. They are usually set on rockwork bases, pierced with small holes in triangular patterns and applied all over with trailing flowers.

Useful wares
The most common useful wares are tea and coffee services.
* Teapots are similar to the Vincennes or Sèvres *théière calabre*. They have ovoid bodies, domed covers and ear-shaped handles, and they are set with tallish, tapered spouts.
* Cups are mostly plain-sided with wishbone, strap handles.
* There are relatively few plates, perhaps because the soft paste tended to warp in the kiln.

These wares, made about 1750, have many typical Mennecy features. The custard pot, *left*, and the pomade pot, *centre*, have the moulded spiral and vertical fluting which was regularly used to break up the shapes.
* The floral decoration on the two pots ignores the fluting.
* The berry knops are very simple.
* The ice cup, *right*, is campana, or bell-shaped and rimmed in puce, which is also the dominant colour in the Mennecy palette.

After 1740 the Rococo style began to replace the Oriental influence. On this eye bath, made around 1750, the Kakiemon palette has been abandoned, and the flowers are European.
* Both the cups *above* and the eye bath would be in Mennecy's distinctive puce rim palette. The early Kakiemon palette was followed by a Rococo palette dominated by puce or pink. The rest of the range was:-
* rich egg-yolk
* pale daffodil
* deep sky blue
* greyish turquoise
* green.

Marks
The Mennecy mark is the letters DV for the Duc de Villeroy, sometimes painted but usually incised, which is very difficult to fake.

VINCENNES AND EARLY SÈVRES

A Vincennes bleu céleste Cuvette Courteille c.1755; ht approx. 8in/20.3cm; value code C

Identification checklist for Vincennes and early Sèvres porcelain

1. Is the porcelain soft-paste?
2. Is the glaze glassy and translucent?
3. Does the enamel appear to sink into the glaze?
4. Is any gilding thick, so that it is easy to feel, and tooled, that is, detailed with lines or other embellishment?
5. If the piece is a figure, is it heavy and pyramid-shaped?
6. Is the piece marked with two interlaced Ls, possibly incorporating a date letter?
7. Is there an additional mark, either initials or a device?

Vincennes (1738-56)

Established as a soft-paste factory in 1738, with the help of craftsmen from Chantilly, Vincennes became the national porcelain factory of France and stylistically one of the most influential in mid-18thC Europe. Although it was at first unsuccessful, its future was secured in 1745, when it was granted a 20-year monopoly to make porcelain in the style of Meissen.

The move to Sèvres

In 1756, the Vincennes factory moved from its original site to the château of Sèvres, near the home of King Louis XV's mistress, Madame de Pompadour, and it was through her influence that the king became sole owner in 1759. In 1769, when a suitable clay was found in France, Sèvres gradually switched to producing hard-paste and in c.1803 finally abandoned the most successful soft-paste formula ever used.

The shape, the heavy mask handles and the extremely detailed, Meissen-style flower painting on this wine glass cooler, made c.1750, show the strong influence of the German factory in the first stages at Vincennes.
* By 1753, this rather ungainly academic style had been replaced by elegant Rococo shapes with flutes and wavy rims.

Wares
The factory concentrated on bowls, potpourri vases, tea sets and dinner services. The earliest wares are entirely derivative, but in the 1740s Vincennes broke away from the Meissen tradition and developed the exuberant and individual style for which it was to become famous. Leading artists, including the goldsmith Jean-Claud Duplessis and the painter François Boucher, were employed to design the shapes and the decorations. Many of the sumptuous Rococo wares reflect the influence of metalwork. But the results are not always harmonious. At times the handles and other appendages look a bit "bolted on". Nevertheless the factory became so successful that its influence can be seen in the products of most of the other European factories, including, ironically, Meissen.

Decoration
The glaze on Vincennes/Sèvres is glassy and translucent. Even more than with other soft-pastes, the warm, lustrous surface is highly receptive to enamelling, which sinks in and merges with it.
* The most popular themes include landscapes, figures, birds and above all, flowers.
* The brushwork is generally freer than on the hard-paste porcelain from German factories.

Ground colours
During the Rococo period a series of brilliant ground colours was introduced to serve as a back-cloth to the representational panels:
* 1749, *bleu lapis* – a rich, almost purple cobalt blue
* 1752, *bleu celeste* – sky blue
* 1753, *jaune jonquille* – a pale lemon-yellow
* 1756, *vert pomme* – mid-green
* 1757, *violette* – violet
* 1758, rose-pink, later incorrectly known as *rose Pompadour*
* 1763, *bleu royal* – a rich enamel blue.

Gilding
The brilliant colours are enhanced by the finest tooled gilding on any porcelain. Except for the work on some of Chelsea's porcelain from the Gold Anchor period (1758-68), almost all other gilding seems flat by comparison.
* Because of the sumptuary laws (see p. 100), other French factories substituted gilding with blue or purple border decoration.

Marks
The pre-revolutionary marks on Vincennes/Sèvres pieces are interlaced Ls (the cipher of Louis XV), which first appeared in underglaze blue in the 1740s.

In 1753 date letters were introduced, (appearing in the space between the Ls), starting with A for 1753 and continuing through to Z for 1777. The year 1778 was then designated by a pair of As, and so on.

In addition, artists signed their work with their own cipher or device. This was usually initials, but occasionally it was a pictogram, such as the running fox of Emile Rénard.

Copies
It is important to remember that the interlaced Ls of Vincennes/Sèvres, together with the crossed swords of Meissen, are by far the most copied marks on European porcelain. Probably more than 90 percent of the interlaced Ls are on later hard-paste copies made in Paris or Limoges. However, relatively few copies have date letters between the Ls.

The Vincennes/Sèvres factory made a handful of figures and groups in unglazed (biscuit) and occasionally glazed porcelain, but the production was very limited compared to wares. The extreme plasticity of the soft-paste meant that figures wilted or collapsed in the heat of the oven. Eventually, the modellers learned to support their figures on large tree-stumps or, like this figure of *Andromeda*, on rocks; and the resulting weight and pyramid shapes contrast dramatically with the lithe, upright figures from Meissen and the other hard-paste factories.

ROYAL SÈVRES

A pair of Sèvres baskets of flowers
c.1760; ht 14in/36cm; value code A

Identification checklist for Sèvres porcelain, 1756-c.1780
1. Is the quality of the gilding exceptional?
2. Is the piece decorated with an identifiable coloured ground (see *previous page*), or with a patterned ground?
3. If the piece is a vessel, does it serve both a practical and a decorative purpose?
4. Have the enamels sunk into the glaze?
5. If the piece is a Rococo figure, is it biscuit?
6. If the piece is a dish or a basin, are the edges lobed?
7. Is the piece decorated with flowers or cartouches of *putti* amid clouds? (But beware Meissen and Derby copies.)
8. Is the mark right? (see *previous page*)

Sèvres, from 1756-c.1780
In the years immediately before and after the move from Vincennes to Sèvres, the French royal porcelain factory made its most complex pieces. During the 1750s and 60s, it employed many of France's finest artists, not only designers and painters but also sculptors, bronze-founders and goldsmiths. The quality control was stricter than at any other factory. Any piece with the slightest warping, pitting or discoloration was rejected. Although many of these "seconds" were somehow smuggled out of the factory and decorated in other workshops, it is unlikely that any of them could be mistaken for the genuine Sèvres. In order to protect his commercial interests, King Louis XV enacted sumptuary laws, which prohibited any other French factory or workshop from using gilding or enamelling.

Range of products
The French use a larger range of tablewares than any other nation, and in the second half of the 18thC the range of wares at Sèvres was correspondingly large. In addition, the factory made pieces which combined a useful and a decorative purpose, such as a pot-pourri and a vase. But it also made decorated and biscuit figures, clockcases and plaques. The plaques were inset in the elaborate furniture of Martin Carlin and Bernard Van Reisenburgh.
* Among the most popular products at this time were the delicate arrangements of model flowers, such as those in the main picture. These were often bought by middlemen known as *marchand-merciers*, who used them to form a setting for Meissen figures, in the same way as bocage was later used in England (see Chelsea, pp. 112-17).

Love, was modelled c.1765 by the great sculptor Etienne-Maurice Falconet, who worked as chief modeller at the factory from 1757 to 1766. Falconet often based his models on his own statues. In this case, he has used a print by the leading French Rococo painter, François Boucher, who also designed decorations for the factory.

In the late 1760s, Sèvres introduced a number of patterned grounds, such as *caillouté* (pebble) and *oeil-de-perdrix* (partridge eye), which was used on this ewer and basin.
* The trophies in the reserve panels were a favourite theme around 1770. Some were painted by Mereaud Buteux, whose father and brother were also decorators at the factory.
* Pear-shaped ewers were made at many 18thC factories, but the Sèvres version has the most elegantly proportioned shape.
* Oval basins were also common, but only Sèvres embellished the line of the edges with lobes.

This pair of *Potpourris Pompadour* were made c.1756 from a drawing now preserved in the factory's archives.
* The shape is thought to have been designed by the leading goldsmith and bronze-founder Jean-Claud Duplessis, who designed many similar vessels for Sèvres.
* The cartouches of *putti* amid clouds were painted by Jean-Louis Morin after a design by Boucher. They were copied at Meissen, and also by Askew at Derby.

The Sèvres factory was the pioneer of "biscuit" (unglazed and undecorated) figures and groups. Without any decorative coating, the models are much crisper, and as the porcelain in this state resembles marble, it became a particularly popular medium for Neo-classical figures. The fashion for biscuit is said to have started when Madame de Pompadour visited the factory to see the progress of some figures. She admired the unfinished models so much that she ordered them to be delivered as they were. This example, called *The Education of*

This vase, in *bleu-du-roi* or *bleu nouveau*, was made c.1770, when the Neo-classical style had become dominant at Sèvres. The panel, decorated in the manner of Viellard, has a Neo-classical oval shape. The gilt swags and trelliswork decorations are very similar to the patterns used for inlays on Neo-classical furniture.
* There are five subtle variations on this shape of Sèvres vase. The earliest was designed in 1756, probably by Falconet, who became chief modeller a year later and was partly responsible for the introduction of Neo-classicism.

POST-REVOLUTIONARY SÈVRES

*A Sèvres footed bowl painted and signed by Langlois
c.1840; dia. 19½in/15cm; value code B*

Identification checklist for post-revolutionary Sèvres
1. Is the porcelain hard-paste? (Soft-paste was used occasionally until c.1800.)
2. Is the mark right (see *opposite* and p. 170)?
3. If visible, is the porcelain body pure white?
4. Are the paste and glaze flawless?
5. Is the gilding very high quality?

Sèvres from c.1780 to 1800
By the time of the French Revolution the factory was producing severely Neo-classical ornaments, including cameos in the style of Wedgwood; and later, under Napoleon, it produced even heavier wares in the style, used also at Berlin, Vienna and Meissen, that was to become known as Empire. Following the Revolution, in 1793, the factory was taken over by the State. The staff was reduced and production nearly came to a standstill. A considerable quantity of porcelain blanks were sold off, and many of these were purchased by English factories and workshops, where they were decorated in the early Sèvres style. Two of the decorators, Thomas Martin and John Randall, specialized in painting birds in the Sèvres style; and they were so good that their work has since caused a lot of confusion.

"Jewel decoration" was introduced at Sèvres in 1781. Thickly applied drops of enamel were used to simulate rubies and emeralds, and as on this cup and saucer, which were made c.1785, drops of porcelain were used to simulate pearls.

New paste and glaze

Sèvres was saved from extinction in 1800, when the arcanist Alexander Brongniart was appointed director. Brongniart reorganized the operation of the factory, abandoned the production of the difficult and expensive soft-paste and invented a new hard-paste, which had ideal plastic qualities, enabling the potters to make massive Neo-classical wares and vases without any fear that they might collapse. The new paste was also capable of carrying the solid ground colours more effectively, and in addition Brongniart developed a range of rich new colours which gave the decorations the deep tone of oil paintings.
* The new paste is close-grained and snow-white and looks like perfect icing (frosting).
* Although the new glaze is slightly grey, it is also very clear, flawless, glassy and translucent.

Marks

From 1793 until 1804, Sevres porcelain is marked "RF" for Republique Française in underglaze blue.
* Between 1800 and 1802, the word "Sèvres" appears alone, either in gold or in colours.
* In 1803 and 4 and perhaps 5, the letters "M.N" and "le" were used, with Sèvres written below. This mark was all in red.
* From 1801, date codes were also used with the ciphers of the kings.

After the introduction of the new hard-paste, Sèvres made a large number of heavily decorated vases in severe Neo-classical shapes, such as this ormolu-mounted example in the shape known as *vase étrusque caraf*, which was made around 1840. The vases are very similar to the contemporary vases made in Vienna and Berlin. They are monumental in form – this one is 17in/43cm tall – and every inch of porcelain is covered in decoration.
* In the mid-19thC there was a widespread fashion for copying the works of well known contemporary artists onto porcelain, and Brongniart's new colours were ideal for this purpose.
* The painter of this "named view", Jean Baptiste Langlace, was the most accomplished decorator working in this field.

Until about 1850, the factory still espoused classical forms and decoration. This service is a little lighter in feel than most, perhaps because of its pale blue ground and the white porcelain which, once again, has been allowed to show through. Dark blue is a much more common ground colour in this period.

PARIS

Part of a Paris dessert service
1815-20; value code A

Identification checklist for Paris porcelain
1. Is the porcelain hard-paste, pure white and flawless?
2. Is the glaze hard and glassy?
3. Does the enamelling sit on the surface of the paste?
4. Is the gilding worn away in places?
5. If the piece is a large vessel, does it have a flared rim?
6. If the piece is a plate, does it have a spur mark in the centre of the base?
7. If the piece is a figure, is it biscuit?
8. Is there a cursive incised mark on the base?

The Paris factories
Towards the end of the 18thC, a large number of high-quality hard-paste factories were established in Paris. With the relaxation of the laws protecting Sèvres, many of their wares were made in imitation of the royal factory, and they were often covered in highly burnished gilding with elaborate designs picked out in matt. However, their porcelain was very resistant to both enamelling and gilt. The decorations seem to sit on the surface and give no sense of having sunk in and become part of the paste, and on most pieces today there are patches where the gilding has worn away. The Paris factories were at their peak in the beginning of the 19thC, when they made severely Neo-classical wares.

As the rents and labour costs in Paris were higher than elsewhere in France, by 1850 most factories had moved to Limoges, where production costs were lower and suitable clay was available nearby. Since then Limoges has been the main centre for the production of porcelain in France.

Paste and glaze

Paris porcelain is a pure white, even and virtually flawless hard-paste.
* The glaze is hard and glassy and rather unsympathetic looking.
* In overall appearance, this white porcelain looks very similar to Nantgarw and Swansea.

On this soup plate from the Denuelle factory, the burnished gilt border has, unusually, survived with no signs of wear. Romantic Middle Eastern figures such as this were popular on Paris plates during the 1820s.
* Most Paris plates were fired on a spur and have a tiny mark on the base.

Many Paris wares were decorated outside the factories. This gold-ground coffee pot, made around 1810, was decorated as far away as Naples, with a very Italian scene – *The Spaghetti Seller.*
* As in this case, Paris coffee pots often have spouts shaped like the heads of birds or animals, usually ducks or dragons.
* Like many tall vessels made by the Paris factories, the pot has a flared rim.

Paris plates made between the end of the revolution and 1830 generally have plain rims. However, during the next ten years some wares began to show the first signs of a Rococo revival. Although the centre of this plate is decorated with a named view enclosed in a Neo-classical gilt roundel, the edge is slightly lobed and the floral reserves on the rims are enclosed in Rococo gilt cartouches.

These pieces from a coffee service made in Paris c.1810, are a good example of the typical combination of severe Neo-classical shapes, which, whenever possible, followed the form of Greek and Etruscan originals, and sensitive and highly accomplished contemporary designs, which usually showed hunting scenes, children at play, or, as here, simple country pursuits.

The Paris factories made very few figures, and most of those that they did make were biscuit. However, at the beginning of the 19thC, biscuit was also used for a number of moulded roundels of the Emperor Napoleon.

HOLLAND

A Weesp tea caddy painted in the Meissen style
c.1765; ht 5¼in/13.3cm; value code F/G

Identification checklist for Dutch porcelain
1. Is the porcelain hard-paste?
2. Is the decoration similar to Meissen?
3. Is the palette dominated by deep pink or purple (Weesp)?
4. Is there a continuous landscape running right round the vessel?
5. Is the decoration in purple *camaïeu*?
6. Are there trailing roots on the underside of the landscape *vignettes*?
7. Is the piece decorated with birds in a palette dominated by brown? (Oude Loosdrecht and Amstel)
8. Are the marks right?

Weesp, Oude Loosdrecht and Amstel (1757-1820)
The first successful Dutch factory was founded at Weesp near Amsterdam in 1757 by an Irish arcanist called D. McCarthy, who had previously worked at Copenhagen. Two years later it was bought by Count Grosveld-Diepenbroick-Impel, who

managed to make hard-paste with the help of a German arcanist, Nikolaus Paul, who later went to Fulda; and in 1771 it was bought by Pastor Johannes de Mol, who moved it to Oude Loosdrecht. After de Mol's death, in 1782, the business was put under the direction of F. Dauber and moved to Amstel, where it remained until it closed in 1820.

Paste and glaze
The paste used at all the Dutch factories is similar to Meissen's hard-paste, but the glaze is duller than Meissen's and less refined.

Wares
While it was at Weesp, the factory made a few figures, modelled by N. Gauron, who had come from Tournai. But at Oude Loosdrecht and Amstel it concentrated entirely on wares. Although they made a few semi-decorative pieces, such as inkstands, the bulk of the factories' output was tea and coffee wares. A lot of white Tournai was decorated at Amstel.
* Coffee pots and teapots have the typical Meissen pear and bullet shapes. Cups and saucers have exactly the same profile as Meissen porcelains. Nevertheless, a few of the more elaborate semi-decorative wares have more individual shapes.
* Tea caddies have sloping or curved shoulders.

Decoration
As with the shapes, decorations also tend to follow Meissen, but the palette is usually dominated by deep pink and purple, the brushwork is more stylized and less precise, and the landscapes sometimes stretch around an entire vessel.

Birds, particularly domestic fowl, were a subject which seems to have appealed particularly to the

Dutch painters. On this Weesp teabowl and saucer, made c.1760, they have been set against a deep pink ground.

This hot-milk jug, made at Oude Loosdrecht c.1775, has a German shape and a loosely painted Meissen-style Chinoiserie design in purple *camaïeu*. But in addition it has one variation which is characteristic of the Dutch factories. Below the figures, there are roots trailing down from the *vignette* in the manner of Fürstenberg or Duvivier.

This Oude Loosdrecht plate, made in the 1770s, is a copy of a Meissen plate decorated by the great Johann Gottlob Hentzschel in the 1740s. The basketweave moulding on the border is broader than on the original, and the birds are more loosely rendered.

Marks
Weesp pieces are either unmarked or else marked in underglaze blue with crossed swords, similar to Meissen's, with three dots in the outer and upper angles. The Oude Loosdrecht mark is "M:O.L." In the final stage, "Amstel" was written out in full.

TOURNAI

*A Tournai group of three children
c.1765; ht 10¾in/27cm; value code F*

Identification checklist for Tournai porcelain
1. Is the porcelain soft-paste?
2. Is the glaze warm with an ivory or grey tinge?
3. If a ware, is it moulded with fine spiral ribs?
4. Is the ware painted *en camaïeu*?
5. If the piece is a figure, is it biscuit or has it been left in the white? (Enamels are rare.)
6. Is the base rockwork?
7. Is the subject romantic?
8. Is the mark right? (see *opposite*)

Tournai (1751-c.1850)

Tournai, the most important factory in the Low Countries, was founded in 1751 by F.J. Peterinck. Two years later, with the help of the arcanist Robert Dubois, who had worked at Chantilly and Vincennes, he began to make soft-paste. After Peterinck's death in 1799, the factory passed to his daughter, who had married the owner of another factory at St-Amand-les-Eaux, but after that it made only useful wares and no figures.

Paste and glaze

Tournai soft-paste was slightly off-white at first and later became ivory-coloured and warmer.

The glaze is soft, translucent and mildly glassy.

Wares

The factory began by imitating Meissen and later, Sèvres. The most characteristic pieces are moulded with spiral panels and basketwork edges, or with very fine spiral ribs, similar to those on Mennecy wares.

Decoration

One of the chief modellers at Tournai was Joseph Willems, who had worked at Chelsea; and the chief decorator was Henri-Joseph Duvivier, who is also thought to have worked in England. Under Duvivier's influence, Tournai decorated many wares with exotic bird patterns, similar to those used at Chelsea and Worcester.

* Tournai made extensive use of monochromes, particularly underglaze blue and overglaze *camaïeu* in rose or puce.
* Many Tournai wares were sold in the white and decorated at The Hague in Holland, where they were usually enamelled with a stork mark.

This plate was painted by Duvivier in c.1765 in puce *camaïeu*. As here, almost all Tournai wares are decorated with vignettes as opposed to framed panels.

* The ozier moulding resembles the Rococo moulding used at Meissen, but the panels are wider.
* Although Tournai was at this time ruled by France, it was able to use gilding in defiance of the sumptuary laws (see p.100), due to the powerful patronage of the Austrian Archduchess, Maria Theresa.

Decorated c.1765 in the manner of Duvivier with scenes from *Aesop's Fables*, which were also used at the Chelsea and Worcester factories, this teabowl and saucer provide a

good example of the stylistic cross-fertilization between Tournai and the leading English factories.

Although Tournai was a large factory with a huge production of table wares and figures, it also produced a limited range of small *galanterien*, such as this snuff box, made c.1770.

Figures

Tournai made a wide range of figures and groups, almost always in contemporary costume. Most were produced in the white or in biscuit after designs by Boucher or Le Creux.

* Groups modelled in the round are perhaps the finest in the Tournai repertoire, and the idea was later taken up at Derby.
* The majority of these figures are mounted on tall rockwork bases with tree stump supports.
* The group in the main picture is a typical example of the massive architectural rockwork and the triangular grouping. There is a considerable loss of detailing, resulting from the thickly applied glaze, which gives the figures a superficial resemblance to those made at Mennecy. The palette, which is a balance of manganese and pink, is very similar to other contemporary French factories.

Marks

The early factory mark is a tower in blue, crimson, gold and sometimes other colours. From c.1765, the mark was clumsily painted crossed swords with crosses in the angles, taken from the arms of the proprietor.

Other Flemish makers

Two minor factories also produced porcelain in the Tournai area: Arras (1770-90) and St-Amand (1771-78). Both made simple blue and white wares similar to Tournai's.

COPENHAGEN

A Copenhagen teapot
c.1780; ht 7⅛in/18cm; value code E

Identification checklist for Copenhagen porcelain
1. Is the porcelain hard-paste?
2. Is the glaze highly refined and virtually flawless?
3. Is the glaze lustrous and slightly greyish?
4. Is the painting meticulous?
5. Does the decoration combine bright colours with muted Neo-classical monochromes?
6. Is the style a mixture of Meissen, Berlin and Sèvres?

Copenhagen (1744-present)
The first porcelain factory in Copenhagen was the soft-paste pottery run by L. Fournier, who had previously worked at Vincennes and Chantilly. C. C. Hunger worked there briefly in the 1730s, and J.C.L. Lück and D. McCarthy came for a while in the 1750s. However, the important factory was the one founded by Frantz Heinrich Muller in 1774 with the queen as his principal shareholder. Five years later it was taken over by the king and became the Royal Danish Porcelain Factory. After several financial setbacks, the crown sold the factory in 1868, but after 1885, when the architect and painter Arnold Krug was appointed artistic director, it underwent a complete renaissance, and has flourished ever since.

Paste and glaze
The hard-paste made by the royal Danish factory is a typical German porcelain, which is usually very neatly potted.

The glaze is highly refined and virtually flawless.

Decoration
In the early phase the influence of other factories, particularly Vienna, Berlin and Sèvres, can be seen in the shapes and decorative designs. Most pieces were severely Neo-classical. Common themes were botanical subjects, figures or topographical views, many painted in monochrome (usually sepia, pink or puce), framed by wreaths or medallions, and occasionally embellished with a scattering of insects and butterflies. The most famous product during the Neo-classical

period was the huge *Flora Danica* botanical dinner service, which had over 1,600 pieces and was made for the Empress of Russia. It was begun in 1790 and not finished until 1802. The next great period was the late 19thC, when the factory produced a famous series of ornamental wares decorated in underglaze smoky blues and greys and strongly influenced by contemporary Japanese wares.

Figures
The Neo-classical, slip-cast figures were mostly based on German and French models, but the factory also made a series of Norwegian peasants, also slip-cast.
* In the mid-19thC the factory produced a series of miniatures based on the sculptures of Thorvaldsen, and at the beginning of the 20thC it produced numerous animals, fish and peasants.

This idiosyncratic angular tray, made c.1780, is painted in characteristic Copenhagen style. The two rather stiff Neo-classical scenes within the medallions are painted in a restrained sepia, but the beribboned swags that separate them are painted in a much brighter palette than most other factories would have used.

Marks
The Copenhagen mark is usually three wavy lines in underglaze blue.

Marieberg
Another leading Scandinavian factory, Marieberg in Sweden, was founded in 1759 by a German, J.L.E. Ehrenreich. With the help of P. Berthevin, a modeller from Mennecy, the factory began to make soft-paste in 1766. It changed to a hybrid hard-paste in 1769, and from 1777 until it gave up making porcelain ten years later, it made a true hard-paste. Marieberg is an extremely rare porcelain.

The Copenhagen factory specialized in making elegant breakfast and tea services which were sold in splendid silk-lined mahogany boxes. In this service, all the pieces have standard Neo-classical forms. The vessels are cylindrical, with angular handles and the centrepiece of each design is a medallion containing one of the puce landscapes which were almost a tradition at Copenhagen.
* In many ways, particularly in the shapes, this service looks as though it could have been made at the Berlin factory, but the blue and gilded borders are more in keeping with Sèvres, and the enthusiastic combination of the two styles could be found nowhere but at Copenhagen.

This Marieberg tea caddy, made in c.1780, is moulded with feathery scrolls in the style of the French Rococo, which was by then somewhat unfashionable in France. Its pastel palette is typical of the factory's early years.

CHELSEA 1: 1745-52

A Chelsea salt, modelled as a crayfish, from a silver original by Nicholas Sprimont c.1745; width 5in/12.7cm; value code C

Identification checklist for Chelsea porcelain, 1745-52
1. Is the porcelain soft-paste?
2. Are there any black "pinholes" on the base?
3. Have the bases of hollow vessels and dishes been ground down?
4. Is the piece shaped like silverware of the day?
5. Are the form and the decoration derived from Meissen?
6. Is the palette predominantly puce, brown and a greenish turquoise (especially 1749-52)?
7. If a figure, is it hollow, and smooth inside?
8. If a vessel, does the piece have chocolate brown rims?
9. Is it marked (see *opposite*)?

Chelsea (1745-69)
The only 18thC English factory to concentrate entirely on luxury porcelain was founded in London in 1745 by Nicholas Sprimont, a Huguenot silversmith from Liège. Because he was aiming his products at "the Quality and Gentry", he opened his factory in Chelsea, close to the fashionable Ranelagh pleasure gardens. The history of the factory divides into four periods, each identified by a different mark.

Incised-triangle, 1745-49
The mark for the earliest period is an incised triangle, although a few of the first pieces are marked with a trident piercing a crown in underglaze blue.

The small-scale table wares produced during this period were predominantly cream jugs, beakers, tea pots and salts. It was Sprimont who introduced the influence of the French Rococo into English porcelain, and the undulating, asymmetrical shapes of these wares reflected the designs he had earlier created in silver.
* Many wares, such as the salt in the main picture, used coral, rocks, shells and crustacea as a decorative theme. Others featured trailing vegetation.
* Crayfish salts were also made at Worcester and the Plymouth and Bristol factories.

Incised-triangle paste
The earliest Chelsea soft-paste is glassy and creamy, like early St Cloud or Mennecy.
* The milk-white glaze is often unevenly applied. It contains a few black "pinholes", and there is sometimes a narrow, unglazed margin around the base of the piece.

Raised-anchor, 1749-52
In 1749 Sprimont moved his factory to new premises and introduced a new mark, an anchor moulded in shallow relief on a small oval pad. With financial backing from Sir Everard Fawkener, who was secretary to the King's brother, the Duke of Cumberland, Chelsea embarked on a brief period of expansion which was to be its most successful both commercially and artistically.

Although the silverware shapes continued, the main influence at Chelsea during the raised-anchor period was Meissen. Many of the Kakiemon shapes and patterns which Meissen had been reproducing since the 1730s were copied in a new formula soft-paste porcelain and decorated using an autumnal palette of puce, brown and greenish turquoise, similar to the palette at Vincennes. On some pieces, such as this chrysanthemum bowl, the Japanese shape is decorated in a European pattern.
* As on most raised-anchor vessels, the rim of the bowl is edged in dark chocolate brown. This was added in imitation of Meissen's version of the Kakiemon style, but on the original the decoration had a practical purpose – the Japanese vessels were rimmed in iron glaze to stop them chipping.
* The most original decorations on raised-anchor wares are the scenes from *Aesop's Fables*, which continued to be used in the red-anchor period and were probably all painted by O'Neale, an artist who later worked at Worcester.

With the help of Sir Everard, who was a friend of the British ambassador in Saxony, the Chelsea modellers borrowed and copied a large number of Meissen figures. Although most of them left the factory white, many were later painted – the best of them, like these goats, in the workshop of William Duesbury (see p.151).
* In addition, the Flemish modeller Joseph Willems modelled a fine series of birds based on the engravings of George Edwards, and also a range of fairly large theatrical, Oriental and contemporary figures based on the engravings of Ravenet, Cochin, Balechou, Aveline and Callot.

Raised-anchor paste
The raised-anchor paste is less glassy than incised-triangle paste, and the milky glaze has a duller and more opaque look, not unlike *faïence*.
* The bases on many wares are covered in an uneven glaze with numerous "pinholes" and a few grey spots in the surface.
* Some wares were very thickly potted, which often made them warp during firing.

Like Japanese porcelain, Chelsea wares were fired on top of three little porcelain spurs, which were usually on the footrim but occasionally on the base. As this allowed glaze to dribble over the foot, the footrims of hollow vessels and dishes were usually ground down after firing.

CHELSEA 2: RED-ANCHOR

*A pair of Chelsea artichoke-tureens and covers
c.1755; ht 9⅛in/23cm; value code C/D*

Identification checklist for Chelsea porcelain, 1752-57
1. Is the porcelain soft-paste?
2. Is the piece decorated in typical red-anchor enamels (see *facing page*)?
3. Does the glaze have a bluish tinge in places where it has pooled?
4. If the piece is shaped like a fruit or a vegetable, is it meticulously modelled?
5. Are the wares decorated in the Meissen or Kakiemon style, or with large-scale botanical specimens?
6. If the piece is a figure, is the decoration very restrained?
7. Is the piece a miniature? (Girl in a Swing factory)
8. If a hollow figure, does it have a smooth interior?

Red-anchor, 1752-57
In 1752 the Chelsea mark changed to a small and neatly pencilled iron-red anchor, usually no more than a quarter of an inch in height. This mark continued until 1757, when Sprimont's illness caused the factory to be closed for several months.

Red-anchor paste
At first red-anchor products were made in the raised-anchor paste, but after about 18 months Sprimont introduced a new formula which was more suited to the elaborate shapes that were then coming into fashion. The new porcelain is translucent and greenish when held to the light.
* The clear glaze often has a bluish tinge in places where it has been too generously applied or has pooled in the angles.

The Meissen style continued to influence Chelsea wares until c.1757, when the more sumptuous Vincennes style began to take over. Like several English factories, Chelsea made baskets in simulated canework, like that *above*, but the detailed moulding and the painted and applied flowers on the Chelsea products are of a much higher quality.

Tureens

It was during the red-anchor period of 1752-57 that Chelsea made its famous Rococo tureens in the shapes of fruit, vegetables and animals. Although the artichoke shape of the tureens in the main picture is unique to the Chelsea factory, many other vegetables, such as cauliflowers, were also made at Worcester and Longton Hall, as well as a number of Continental factories. However, it is the Chelsea modelling and painting that stand out as the most meticulous.

The most famous of all Chelsea's red-anchor products are the "Hans Sloane" wares – so called because their decorations were said to represent botanical specimens from Sir Hans Sloane's Chelsea Physic Garden and were based on engravings by the curator, Philip Miller, and Georg Dionysius Ehret. The specimens take up most of the surface of the wares and are painted in great detail and on a much larger scale than the flowers and plants on any other wares. On the other hand, Bow's botanical wares are generally of inferior workmanship.
* Many plates are populated by winged insects, bugs and butterflies; and these, together with the plants, are often given shadowed outlines in the manner of J.G. Klinger of Meissen.
* This plate contains all the colours of the red-anchor palette.

Chelsea's red-anchor figures are influenced by Meissen, but they lack movement, and the heavy glaze makes them less severe. As can be seen from this ostler, modelled by Joseph Willems around 1755, the colouring is much more subdued than on figures from other

English factories, and the features are much more detailed.
* The pad base follows Meissen, but as it is soft-paste, the edge has become discoloured.

"Girl in a Swing"

During the 1750s there was a second porcelain factory in Chelsea, run by modellers and painters who had previously worked for Sprimont. Known as the "Girl in a Swing" factory after one of its earliest figures, it concentrated on miniatures.

The tiny figures, most of which are in the white like those *below*, are wonderfully angular and unlike anything from any other English factory.
* Apart from figures and snuff boxes, the "Girl in a Swing" factory made the first porcelain

"toys" in England. Most of them were delicate miniature wares, almost always decorated with flowers.
* The factory is now known to have been under the management of Charles Gouyn. It was situated in St. James's, at the heart of fashionable London, and made delicately enamelled tea wares in addition to the miniature "toys".

CHELSEA 3: GOLD-ANCHOR

A Chelsea gold-anchor scent flask
1760-5; ht 7in/17.8cm; value code E/F

Identification checklist for Chelsea gold-anchor porcelain, 1759-69

1. Is the porcelain soft-paste and comparatively opaque?
2. Is the glaze thick and bluish?
3. Does the glaze have a wide crackle (see *below*)?
4. Are wares extensively covered in high quality gilding?
5. If the ground is dark blue or claret, is it very patchy?
6. If the piece is a figure, does it have a small head?
7. Is it very elaborately decorated?
8. Is it set on a symmetrical Rococo-scroll base?
9. Is the base enclosed (unlike early Chelsea)?

Gold-anchor, 1759-69

In 1759, when Nicholas Sprimont recovered from his illness, the Chelsea factory reopened with a new mark – a thick gold anchor – signifying a complete change in taste. German restraint gave way to the French flamboyance of Vincennes and Sèvres. For the last ten years of its independence, before it was taken over by William Duesbury of Derby, Chelsea made wares and figures in the high Rococo style.

Paste and glaze

The exuberant Rococo modelling was made possible by the use of a new paste formula, containing bone ash, which could be thickly potted and tended to result in heavier, more opaque wares. However, the advantages of the new paste were partly counteracted by the new glaze, which was thick and bluish. It tended to produce wide, irregular crackles and often formed large globules on the base.

Decoration
The designs on gold-anchor wares are painted in a bright palette. In most cases they are set against solid coloured grounds embellished with rich gilding. Judging by decoration alone, many pieces could be mistaken for Vincennes or Sèvres, but they are often betrayed by their profiles and over-elaborate moulding. The self-conscious handles on the scent flask in the main picture could never have been made at one of the sophisticated French factories. The most common grounds are:
* deep Mazarin blue, presumably based on Sèvres' *bleu lapis*.
* claret, which was an unsubtle attempt to copy *rose Pompadour*.

The quality of Chelsea's gilding was the closest to Sèvres'. On many pieces, such as this extravagant vase, made around 1765, the gilding was used to disguise the patchiness of the difficult ground colour, which has also drifted onto the parts of the feet which were left white.

Many Chelsea wares were decorated outside the factory. These *potpourri* vases, made around 1765, were painted in the London workshop of James Giles. The exotic birds, derived directly from Sèvres, are painted much more loosely than they are on the Sèvres originals.
* Like many Chelsea pieces of this period, the vases are heavily encrusted with flowers.

Figures
Gold-anchor figures are as elaborate as the wares. Like French figures, most are inspired by prints, but where the French modellers remained faithful to the originals, Chelsea modellers embellished them. For example, their groups were often swamped by flowery settings. The technique of building up models with encrusted flowers and leaves, known as bocage, originated at Chelsea in the gold-anchor period. Although the device was later copied by most English factories, it was never used anywhere else in Europe.
* When the bocage was used as a backdrop, the groups were designed to be displayed on a shelf, and some are marked on the undecorated back instead of the base.
* Figures tend to have disproportionately small heads.

Bases
Gold-anchor figures have high, pierced, scroll bases, heightened with gilding and encrusted with applied flowers. However, unlike all other Rococo bases, the Chelsea versions are symmetrical.

Like the purely decorative figures, sweetmeat figures are encrusted with flowers and set on symmetrical Rococo bases.

BOW

Bow figures
c.1760; ht approx. 8in/20.3cm; value code D

Identification checklist for Bow porcelain
1. Is the paste white and chalky?
2. Is the glaze greenish and glassy?
3. If the piece is decorated in polychrome, do the colours include sky-blue, egg-yolk yellow and puce?
4. If the piece is a ware, is it decorated in an Oriental style?
5. If the piece is a figure, is it press-moulded (see p. 12) and rather heavy?
6. Has the figure been left in the white (pre-1755)?
7. Has the thick glaze obscured some of the modelling?

Bow (1744-75)

Founded by Thomas Frye and Edward Heylyn in 1744, Bow was much less exclusive than the other great London factory, Chelsea. It made wares and figures for a much wider market, and grew to become the largest factory in England, but after 1760 it declined, and was finally sold off in 1775.

Paste and glaze

Bow paste is white and chalky with an open, granular texture and an irregular surface.

The glaze is glassy, greyish or greenish and has a tendency to peppering or crackling.

Palette

Bow used many colours, but the three which dominated the palette in the mid-1750s were:
* milky, deep sky-blue
* rich, egg-yolk yellow
* deep, purplish puce.

Figures

Bow figures were press-moulded rather than slip-cast. This gave them a much heavier body, and in order to prevent them collapsing during firing, they were constructed almost architecturally. They were also covered in a heavy glaze, which tended to obscure the details.

Most of the early Bow figures were left in the white. Apart from subjects borrowed from Meissen or based on Oriental models, the most popular figures were portraits of theatrical personalities, such as this model of the English actress Kitty Clive, made around 1750.
* Note the clumsy modelling.

By c.1755, the figures were well coloured in the characteristic Bow enamels. But they still stood on relatively simple mound bases, which were sometimes applied with flowers. However, after 1760 bases were moulded in the Rococo style and were often elevated on high scroll feet, like those in the main picture.

* Just as at Chelsea, the Bow modellers had a tendency to be over-elaborate and use overpowering tree-stump supports laden with blossom.
* Many of the later figures are relatively poorly modelled and far inferior to the Derby products of the same period.

Wares
Almost all Bow wares were based on Oriental designs. The initial output consisted of two types:-
1. *Blanc-de-Chine*-style wares, with the sides of vessels and dishes moulded in shallow relief with pine, *prunus* or bamboo.
2. Underglaze blue designs taken from both China and Japan.
* Even the later enamelled wares were based on *famille rose* or, more commonly, Kakiemon designs.

This very early blue and white inkwell is marked "Made at New Canton", which was the name of the Bow factory. The patches of rusty colour breaking through in places where the granular body has absorbed moisture are also found on Lowestoft and Derby.

Some heavily potted tureens in this bulbous shape have a lion finial instead of this twig knop.
* The decoration – a European version of a *famille rose* pattern – was used at Bow between 1750 and 60.
* Bow used an anchor and dagger mark as well as a wide range of other devices.

119

WORCESTER 1

A moulded transfer printed Worcester "cabbage leaf" jug c.1760-65; ht 9in/23cm; value code E/F

Identification checklist for Worcester porcelain from 1752 to c.1774
1. Is the paste greenish in transmitted light?
2. Are there isolated areas containing tiny, peppery pinpricks?
3. Is there an unglazed margin inside the footrim?
4. Is the piece moulded?
5. Is it decorated with underglaze transfer printing?
6. Is the ground colour "wet", or painted in scales?
7. Do the grounds contain vase- or mirror-shaped panels surrounded by Rococo gilt frames?
8. Are the marks right? (see *opposite*)

Worcester, from 1751-c.1774
The Worcester factory was founded on June 4, 1751, by a group of 15 gentlemen, merchants and craftsmen, including Dr John Wall, who managed it until 1774. In 1752, the factory bought out Benjamin Lund's Bristol factory. By combining Dr Wall's soft-paste formula with Bristol's experience and technical expertise, Worcester was soon manufacturing a surprisingly sophisticated range of products.

Soft-paste

Early Worcester porcelain contained soapstone, which enabled it to withstand boiling water. This made it particularly suitable for the tea and coffee wares which the factory produced in large quantities.
* The body has a greenish tinge, which can be easily seen when the piece is held up to the light, and there are often small, isolated patches of tiny, peppery pinpricks.
* The greenish or bluish glaze is close-fitting and free from crackle.

Moulding

Early Worcester wares were invariably thinly potted. As a result, most large pieces tended to warp or sag. The moulded surfaces helped to disguise flaws in the glaze. The most famous example of this moulding is the "cabbage leaf" pattern used on the jug in the main picture.

"Pegging"

All Worcester products have a narrow, unglazed margin round the interior of the footrim. This was caused by a process known as "pegging", which was originally designed to prevent any of the thick excess glaze from spilling over onto the kiln furniture while the piece was being fired. Before the firing began, the excess glaze was scraped away from the inner footrim with a wooden peg.

Sauceboats are among the most common early Worcester products. Most, like this example, are decorated in a monochrome underglaze blue, which can vary from a soft, greyish blue to a deep, almost black cobalt.

Transfer printing

Worcester was one of the pioneers of overglaze transfer printing, as on the cabbage jug in the main picture. However, in 1760 it began to switch to underglaze printing, which ensured that the print did not wear off.

This moulded hexagonal cream jug has many features typical of early Worcester:
* it is quite small – few early wares are more than 6in (15cm) high
* the overall shape is derived from silverware
* the ear-shaped handle with a high scrolled thumbpiece looks a bit like a script "3".
* the tentative Chinoiserie decorations are painted in a bold hybrid palette drawn from both *famille verte* and *famille rose*
* the inside of the rim is decorated with small ribboned objects
* the moulding is enhanced by the bright sparkle of the glaze.

In the late 1760s, the painting of Chinoiserie and flower decorations became more confident, and a new, more opulent Sèvres style emerged. Panels containing flowers and exotic birds were surrounded by Rococo, honey-gilded frames and set against bold ground colours, such as the "wet blue" on this cup and saucer.

Marks

From the 1760s onwards, Worcester marked its wares with a crescent in underglaze blue. This was copied at Lowestoft and should also not be confused with the "C" of Caughley.

WORCESTER 2

Part of a Worcester crested dessert service c.1770; value code C

Identification checklist for Worcester porcelain from c.1774 to c.1810
1. Is the porcelain soft-paste?
2. Is the paste greyish but refined looking:
3. Is the decoration very restricted?
4. Is the palette predominantly gilding with puce, blue or brown?
5. Do the pieces have severely Neo-classical shapes? (See *opposite*.)
6. Do the smaller vessels have handles shaped like Irish harps?
7. Are the knops on the pots shaped like mushrooms with tight, upturned leaves around them?
8. Is the mark right? (See *opposite*.)

Worcester from c.1774-c.1810
After Dr. Wall retired, in 1774, his factory was managed by another partner, William Davis, until it was bought by its London agent, Thomas Flight, in 1783. Three years later his chief decorator, Robert Chamberlain, left to form a rival firm, first decorating porcelain from Caughley and then producing his own hybrid hard-paste. Within a decade there were two thriving Worcester firms. Meanwhile the original firm was going through several changes of name. After Flight's death, in 1792, his two sons went into partnership with Martin Barr and began to trade as Flight & Barr, and in 1807, when they were joined by another Barr, their firm's name became Barr, Flight and Barr. During these years, the first factory's wares were unsurpassed. Many of the leading English decorators worked there; and, most unusually, they were paid by the hour and not by the piece.

Paste and glaze
Under Thomas Flight's management, the soft-paste became a more brilliant hard-paste, the glaze became more refined and the potting became more even and a little thicker. However, both glaze and body maintained their overall greyish appearance.

Figures
The new paste was much more suitable for modelling than the earlier one, which had been used to produce only a few rather "wooden" figures, but by the time it arrived the factory's reputation for wares was well established and figures remained a rarity.

Towards Neo-classicism
Throughout the 1770s the factory continued to make brilliantly coloured Rococo ground wares, but at the same time the Neo-classical influence became stronger and stronger. The ground

colours retreated to the rims of the wares, where they were often heavily gilded. The vase and mirror-shaped frames round the reserves became simple circles and ovals. The colourful scattered sprays of flowers gave way to isolated gilt sprigs. Soon the only remnant of the Rococo was the shape of some of the plates and dishes.

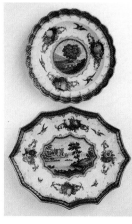

These dishes, from a service made for Lord Henry Thynne date to c.1770 – the same date as the Rococo sucrier on p. 121, but despite the similarity in shape and the use of strong colours, the theme here is Neo-classical.

At the end of the 18thC, the shapes of Worcester tea and coffee wares were usually severely Neo-classical. These pieces from a tea service made around 1795 have several of Worcester's typical Neo-classical features:
* the teapot has fluting round the shoulders
* the knop is shaped like a small mushroom surrounded by small stiff leaves pointing upwards
* the vessels have the profile of a truncated shield
* the handle on the cup is a simple circle and the handles on the pot

and sucrier are shaped like an Irish harp
* on each piece, much of the surface has been left white. The decoration is now very simple and would have been painted in the restricted Neo-classical palette of brown and gilding, although blue and puce with gilding are more common.
* The Worcester factory also applied a strict, almost architectural Neo-classicism to the production of a large number of extremely elegant decorative wares. These include:-
* conical bough pots
* *cassolettes*
* *potpourri* jars
* spill-holders
* inkwells.

At the beginning of the 19thC, Worcester wares began to throw off the disciplined austerity of Neo-classicism and embrace the light-hearted extravagance that was to become a hallmark of the Regency taste. This teapot, made c.1805, still has the truncated-shield profile, but there is now a broad gallery-like peak above the spout, the decoration is much more exuberant, and it has been painted in a broader, livelier palette.

Marks
During Thomas Flight's management, many Worcester pieces were marked simply with the name "Flight", painted in script in underglaze blue.
* From 1793 until around 1811, pieces were marked with an incised "B" for Martin Barr.
* The name "Flight & Barr" was also painted in blue, red or gold script.
* After 1807, the letters "B F B", for Barr, Flight and Barr, were both painted and incised.
* At the same time, wares from the rival factory were appearing with the mark "Chamberlains Worcester" in red or purple script.

123

A Barr, Flight & Barr bough pot
c.1810; ht 7½in/19.7cm; value code D/E.

Identification checklist for Worcester porcelain from 1810 to 1840

1. Is the porcelain hard-paste?
2. If the piece is part of a dinner or dessert service, is the porcelain hard, white and translucent, with a glassy glaze? (Other wares have the greyish look of other early Worcester, see p. 122.)
3. Is the gilding of an unusually high quality?
4. Is the decoration of the panels extremely detailed and exact?
5. If the piece is a plaque, does it have an extravagant gilt frame?
6. If a Rococo plate, does the piece have only six bracket lobes on the rim?
7. If a vessel, does it have angular handles and loop knops on its cover?
8. If a cup, is it a severe bucket-shape?

Worcester from 1810-40

When Martin Barr died in 1813 the old Worcester firm changed its name again, this time to Flight, Barr & Barr. The styles continued uninterrupted and the quality improved still further, but at the same time the rival factory of Chamberlain's was flourishing.

In 1840, Chamberlain's took over Flight, Barr & Barr, and in 1852 Chamberlain's was itself bought out by the partnership of Kerr and

Binns. Ten years later the new owners formed the Worcester Royal Porcelain Company, which survives to this day. Meanwhile, a third factory had been established in Worcester. In 1800, Thomas Grainger, a relation of Chamberlain, established a firm which became known as Grainger, Lee and Co., which continued trading until the end of the 19thC imitating Chamberlain's products and reproducing Wall's early wares.

Neo-classicism

In the early part of the 19thC, Neo-classicism remained the dominant theme at the factory run by the Barr and Flight families, but the decorations became progressively less restrained. Table wares were produced and, to a lesser extent, mantelshelf pieces. The D-shaped bough pot in the main picture has many of the factory's typical Neo-classical features: the lines are cleanly classical with no fanciful interpretations, whilst the almost photographic decoration of the panels is emphasized by rectangular frames and pilasters. The base frieze is painted with stylized palms and foliage, which is typical of all early 18thC English factories, but the quality of the Worcester gilding is much finer. Only Swansea and Nantgarw come close to it, and their decoration is usually less meticulous. The ground colour for the base frieze and the top is salmon-pink, one of the factory's favourite colours. The others were:
* orange
* grey marbling.

In the early 19thC, at almost ruinous expense, Chamberlain's developed a fine, hard, white, very translucent porcelain covered in a glassy, Paris-type glaze. Known as "Regent China", it was used almost exclusively for dinner and dessert services, such as this one, made around 1815. The Rococo-shaped plates, which reflect the Sèvres style of the 1760s, have much in common with plates from other British factories, but there are some subtle differences between them.
* the kidney-shaped dish has a more complex wavy rim than the equivalent dish from Coalport or Spode
* the essentially Rococo decoration also includes Neo-classical features, such as festoons and swags.

Napoleon's campaigns in Egypt and Nelson's victory on the Nile led to a brief fashion for the Egyptian style, which reached its height around 1810, when this chocolate cup was made. The unlikely combination of an Egyptian theme with Neo-classical shapes and borders is typical of most factories, but there are several features which distinguish this cup as late Barr, Flight & Barr:
* the severe bucket-shape of the cup itself
* the angular handles and the loop knop
* the quality of painting, unequalled in England or Wales at the time and comparable with the best in Europe.

Chamberlain decorated a number of his wares with topographical scenes of Malvern. These became so popular that he also issued similar plaques surrounded by extravagant gilt frames.
* Plaques were more popular among European factories than other British factories, but none were framed so flamboyantly.

Marks

Each Worcester factory used its name as a mark. The Flight, Barr & Barr name was often printed, with the royal coat of arms and the London address, or painted in script. Chamberlain's name was painted in script or capitals, usually in red or purple, or impressed in Roman letters, whilst "Grainger, Lee & Co." was usually painted in red script.

125

LOWESTOFT

A Lowestoft blue and white bottle
1764; ht 10-12in/25.4-30.5cm; value code B

Identification checklist for Lowestoft porcelain
1. Is the porcelain soft-paste?
2. Is there any brownish discolouration?
3. If the piece is decorated in underglaze blue, is the blue slightly blurred and greyish?
4. Is the glaze greenish or greyish, and has it pooled to a more intense colour in crevices?
5. If the piece is a coffee cup or pot, does the handle have a kick-back terminal on the lower joint?
6. If the piece is a cup, does it have a conical base and a wedge-shaped footrim?
7. Is there an underglaze blue numeral inside the foot?

Lowestoft (1757-c.1800)
The Lowestoft factory was founded in 1757 by Robert Browne and three partners. Situated in a remote fishing port on the coast of Suffolk, it was a long way from the fashionable marketplaces and it was completely out of touch with changing tastes, but it survived for almost 50 years at a time when Chelsea, Bow, Derby and Worcester were at their peak.

Paste and glaze
Lowestoft is a phosphatic porcelain, similar to Bow, with a tendency to discolouration. The glaze is not particularly glassy and has a slightly greenish or greyish tone, which pools to a more intense colour in crevices.

Wares
All the wares made during the factory's first ten years are decorated in a cold underglaze blue which varies from a greyish to an almost black tone. The influence of Worcester is often obvious, not only in the Chinoiserie designs but also in the moulded decorations, but the actual shapes of the wares were usually derived from saltglaze stoneware. From the mid-1760s overglaze colours and underglaze blue printing were introduced

126

but, apart from some of the floral themes, the designs were seldom as charming as the earlier blue versions.
* Dishes and bowls were often fired on three tiny spurs, which left splinter-like scars on the thin wedge-shaped footrims.
* A special feature of the factory was its commemorative wares, made to order to commemorate a birthday or a marriage.
* Other wares made at Lowestoft which were unusual elsewhere were: pap warmers, feeding cups and flasks.
* The factory also made a number of now very rare figures, usually somewhat primitive and depicting cats, sheep, pugdogs, *putti* and musicians.

* The design also suffers from the slightly blurred effect that distinguishes Lowestoft, especially on its copies of the much more precise Worcester patterns.

In both shape and style this teapot is based very closely on a typical piece of Chinese *famille rose* export ware from the 1760s. The Lowestoft copies of these wares were so good that until quite recently many experts were ascribing large numbers of perfectly acceptable Chinese export wares to the Suffolk factory. In one of the first books written about Lowestoft, several of the illustrations show pieces which are now known to be Chinese.

This teapot, made between 1775 and 1780, is decorated in underglaze blue, iron-red and gilding – the usual Imari colours. The shapeless arrangement of rocks and vegetarian is typical of the Lowestoft naïveté.
* The design is called the Redgrave "two bird" pattern, after the family who gave their name to the Imari palette at Lowestoft.

This pear-shaped coffee pot, with its exaggeratedly tall dome cover and kick-back handle, has a pattern that is unique to Lowestoft. It is known as the Robert Browne pattern, after the founding partner, who was also the factory's first manager.

Marks
Lowestoft wares carry no marks other than the crescents on copies of Worcester wares. However, most underglaze blue and some coloured wares pre-1770s have numerals on the inside of the footrim.

This dish is unusual in that it is painted in underglaze blue with an Italianate landscape vignette, rather than a Chinoiserie design.
* The greenish glaze shows particularly in the well of the dish; and the upper rim has the discolouring which is very common at this factory.
* This dish and the bottle in the main picture are good examples of the wide variations in underglaze blue at Lowestoft.

LIVERPOOL

*A Christian's Liverpool vase
1765; ht 3⅜in/8.5cm; value code E.*

Identification checklist for Liverpool porcelain
1. Has the paste discoloured?
2. Is the glaze bluish or greenish?
3. Are there areas of peppering?
4. Is the decoration blue and white Chinoiserie?
5. Is the cobalt inky black?
6. Is the appearance like a greyish early Worcester?
7. Are there tiny areas of iridescence?
8. If the piece is a bowl, is the footrim undercut?
9. If the piece is a teapot or coffee can, is the footrim wedge-shaped?
10. Does the painting look clumsy?
11. If the decoration is printed, does it look primitive?

Liverpool

There were several small porcelain factories in Liverpool in the second half of the 18thC, but there are so few records that it is often impossible to attribute pieces to specific factories. However, it is known that most of the factories used a soaprock porcelain, like that used at Worcester and Caughley. The greyish appearance of most Liverpool porcelain is in fact very similar to Worcester's, but it tends to suffer from peppering and the potting is variable. Figures are rare. The most popular products are blue and white tea and coffee services. But decorators also used enamels, either in a style similar to Worcester's, or else in a harsh *famille rose* palette, which can be confused with New Hall or even Lowestoft.
* Wares are unmarked except for a few spurious Worcester crescents.
* The main factories were: Richard Chaffer (1754-65), Philip Christian (1765-76), Samuel Gilbody (c.1754-61), William Reid and others (c.1755-70), John and Jane Pennington (c.1770-94), Seth Pennington and John Part (1778-1803).

* Chaffer's wares are usually very translucent and almost white, and they appear slightly green when held up to a strong white light.
* The phosphate in the porcelain formula has caused discolouration in areas where the glaze is thin.

These are three examples from different Liverpool factories. They all have the general greyish look of Liverpool porcelain, although the Pennington's teabowl (*top right*) is slightly warmer.
* There is peppering on the base of the Christian's bowl (*above bottom*).
* The blue and white Chaffer's cup (*top left*) has a greyish blue body and a unique quilted design but the dark cobalt blue is typical of most Liverpool factories.
* All three have a bluish glaze which has gathered in very dark pools on the inside of their footrims.

This early Christian's tea caddy has the slightly bluish glaze typical of Liverpool porcelain, especially where it has gathered near the shoulder.
* The piece is made out of a chalky, plaster-like paste which was typical of Christian's factory.
* The delicately painted enamels are not unlike those used at Worcester in the 1750s.

This is an extremely rare Chaffer's figure of a nun, made in the late 1750s. It was intended to represent the tragic figure of Heloise, the lover of Abelard.
* Similar figures were made at Longton Hall, Bow and Chelsea.

The very meticulous pseudo-Chinese painting on this Christian's mug of 1775, is typical of Liverpool's porcelain (and delftware). There is some peppering around the base.
* Many Christian's wares have a wedge-shaped footrim with a flat base like this one. As here, there is often discolouring on the rim.

The Chaffer's tankard is naïvely painted in *famille rose* colours, with the factory's usual egg-yolk yellow and mushroom pink.

The typical handle found on Liverpool's vessels has a large, curling projection on the upper curve.

PLYMOUTH AND CHAMPION'S BRISTOL

A Plymouth bell-shaped mug in a famille rose *palette c.1770; ht 7in/17.8cm; value code E/F*

Identification checklist for Plymouth and Champion's Bristol porcelain

1. Is the porcelain hard-paste and greyish?
2. Are figures press-moulded?
3. Is the glaze yellowish?
4. Are there dark, smoky patches?
5. If the piece is a ware, is it a Rococo shape with Neo-classical decorations?
6. Do small hollow wares have elaborately moulded cartouches?
7. If the piece is a figure, is it heavy and does it look as though it has sagged or split in places?
8. If the figure is a man, does it have a feminine face?
9. Are the marks right?

Plymouth (1768-70)
Established in 1768 by a chemist, William Cookworthy, Plymouth and Cookworthy's Bristol were the first English factories to make true hard-paste porcelain. Plymouth produced the usual range of wares, decorated in either underglaze blue or polychrome enamels,

and a range of naïve, massively-modelled figures with splits in their sides. Almost every product had a flaw, and so in 1770 Cookworthy moved his factory to the important ceramics centre of Bristol (Cookworthy's Bristol 1770-74), where it was easier to find an experienced workforce.

This Plymouth cream jug has a characteristically "old-fashioned" Rococo shape and typically tentative enamelling.
* The moulded cartouches are among the most elaborate on any English porcelain.
* Unusually, the glaze does not suffer from darkening, although it has a characteristic yellowness.

Champion's Bristol (1774-81)

In 1774 Cookworthy assigned his factory to a young Quaker, Richard Champion, who introduced designs and shapes in the Neo-classical taste. However, the factory never knew financial stability and closed in 1781. The patent passed to New Hall (see pp.132-33).

Paste and glaze

Both factories used a greyish-white paste with a cold, glassy, yellowish glaze. On larger pieces it tended to sag or split in the kiln, but at Bristol there was less darkening caused by misfiring.

Champion's Bristol figures are relatively large. This emblem of *Autumn* is 10in/25.4cm tall. Although physically strong-looking, it has a typically characterless and almost feminine face, very like the figures modelled by Wenzel Neu at Closter-Veilsdorf.
* The rockwork bases on these figures were usually washed in a vibrant green and edged in yellow and russet.

On this early Champion's Bristol cup and cream jug, made around 1775, the double-ogee late-Rococo shapes conflict with the Neo-classical decoration.
* The gilding on Champion's wares from this period is of a very high quality.

The ear-shaped handle with a "wishbone" projection at the bottom was used on many Bristol teapots and larger vessels in the mid-1770s.

Plymouth bell-shaped tankards, such as the one in the main picture, became so popular in the 19thC that a number of fakes were produced both in England and in France. This fake carries the Plymouth mark, but the paste has no greyish tone, the palette is completely different, and the attempt to re-create the bird patterns of Plymouth's great decorator Michel Soqui is much too loose and lacks detail.

Marks

The mark used only at Plymouth was a combination of 2 and 4, the alchemical sign for tin, which was the main product of Cornwall before Cookworthy found the china clay which was soon to be used by every English factory.
 The Bristol mark is a simple cross in overglaze blue, sometimes accompanied by a "B", or else the crossed swords of Meissen in underglaze blue.

131

NEW HALL

*New Hall wares decorated by Fidèle Duvivier
c.1785; value code E*

Identification checklist for New Hall porcelain
1. Is the glaze thick, dull and greenish?
2. Are there any pools in the glaze and are they filled with small bubbles?
3. Are the wares fluted or moulded?
4. Are the shapes similar to those used by Worcester or Caughley?
5. Is puce prominent in the palette?
6. Is the piece decorated in the manner of late Chinese export ware?

New Hall (1781–c.1812)
The second Staffordshire porcelain factory (Longton Hall was the first) was founded by a group of local potters who bought Richard Champion's patent for hybrid hard-paste in 1781. After operating briefly and unsuccessfully at Tunstall, they moved to nearby Shelton in 1782, and it was this second factory which became known as New Hall.

Paste and glaze
As it is made to the same formula, the greyish New Hall paste is inevitably very similar to Champion's Bristol paste, and the wares suffers from many of the same weaknesses, such as wreathing.
The glaze, on the other hand, is completely different. Thick, dull and greenish, it sometimes leaves areas uncovered, and it tends to gather in pools which are filled with little bubbles.

Wares
The New Hall factory made no figures and very few decorative wares. The majority of its products are tea wares, and apart from these it seems to have made some dessert wares, jugs and punch bowls.

Shapes and decoration
In the early phase of production, up until about 1800, most wares were fluted or moulded in shapes very similar to those used at Worcester and Caughley. However, despite the Neo-classical shapes, the decorations often followed the designs of late Chinese export ware, particularly *famille rose* flower patterns and figure subjects, which were usually printed and then colour washed. The finest and rarest of the early wares, such as those in the main picture, were decorated by the French artist Fidèle Duvivier, who was known

particularly for his landscapes.
Later wares followed the Neo-
classical shapes and designs used
by many other factories, but there
was also one decorative technique
which was unique to New Hall.
Known as Warburton's patent
after one of the founding partners,
it was used for painting scenes in
on-glaze gold.

This teapot is typical of the first
phase of production at the New
Hall factory. The basic silver-
shape was copied by several other
factories, but the edges detailed in
enamel (usually puce or blue), the
flowers with dotted heads and the
fan-like motifs in the frieze are
characteristic New Hall
decorations.
* Some of these early teapots
have little feet shaped like
rosettes.

This teapot, which was made soon
after 1810, represents the second
and much more sophisticated
phase of production at New Hall.
Many factories used this high-
galleried, Neo-classical silver
shape; and the underglaze blue
panels at either end, delicately
painted in gilt with palmettes and
fern-like vegetation, were a very
popular form of decoration. But
there are two features of this
teapot which are unique to New
Hall:
* the knop modelled in the form
of a Chinese hat is particularly
characteristic
* the scene on the side has been
applied using Warburton's patent,
but, as with most examples of this
technique, the gold has faded over
the years and lost its crispness, and
has now become a drab brown.

In c.1812 the New Hall factory
converted from hard-paste to bone
china. This bone china egg cup,
made c.1815, is painted in the
bright palette that was also used at
Spode, Coalport and many other
factories, but as always in New
Hall flower patterns, the central
flower is a large rose.

Marks
A few bone china wares bear the
printed mark "New Hall"
surrounded by two circles.
* Earlier wares have no factory
mark, but the large pieces in
services are marked with the letter
"N" followed by a pattern number
below 1940, usually in red.

Davenport (1794-1887)

Another important Staffordshire
factory was the one run by John
Davenport at Longport. Originally
an earthenware pottery, it began
to make hard-paste bulb pots and
bone china wares c.1800, and from
about 1812 onwards it
concentrated on bone china tea
and dessert services. At the
beginning of the 19thC the factory
was very fashionable and
numbered the Prince Regent
among its customers.
* Davenport decoration is of a
very high standard. The painters
often imitated Derby, but they
also developed designs of their
own, including Imari patterns.

COALPORT

Coalport Neo-rococo vase
c.1835; ht 11⅛in/28.2cm; value code E/F

Identification checklist for Coalport porcelain
1. Is the piece a greyish hybrid hard-paste (pre-1820)?
2. Is the glaze dull and grainy?
3. Is the piece made of fine white bone china (post-1820)?
4. Is it liberally encrusted with flowers?
5. If a plate, does the rim have six lobes with shallow notches?
6. Is the piece decorated in a bright Imari palette?
7. Does it have a fractional pattern number?

Coalport (1790-present)
The Coalport factory in Shropshire was founded in the 1790s by John Rose, who later bought Caughley and Nantgarw. Now housed at Stoke-on-Trent, the factory is still in production.

Paste and glaze
Until 1820 the factory made a greyish hybrid hard-paste, similar to New Hall's, and covered it with a dull grainy glaze.
* After 1820 it made a fine

quality white bone china similar to that used at Minton.

Wares
Coalport concentrated on table and decorative wares.
* In the 1870s it began to make the flower-encrusted Rococo pieces for which it was to become famous, and after the Great Exhibition in 1851 it produced a large number of Sèvres-style vases with *bleu celeste* or *rose Pompadour* grounds.

Decoration

The most prominent among the many decorative themes are:-
* Neo-classical designs with the emphasis on a drab or restricted palette
* Imari patterns
* delicate bouquets of summer flowers dominated by pink.
* Landscape views, which were rarely named.

Ground colours

The most popular ground colours on services are:-
* apple green
* dark blue
* beige.

Marks

Early pieces were not marked, but some later wares were marked with a script "Coalport"; and many of the Rococo and flower-encrusted vases were marked "Coalbrookdale".
* Pattern numbers were used after c.1820.

ground more characteristic of the early stages of the factory, but the shape is very typical, and so too are the entwined stalk knop and the flaring Sèvres-type foliate handles.

Both Coalport and Minton made reproductions of earlier styles, which they represented to their customers as minor works of art. The conflicting mixture of a classical Sèvres shape and Mannerist entwined snakes on this vase with a *bleu celeste* ground, dated 1871, is very typical of late 19thC Coalport.

These pieces, made between 1800 and 1805, are composed of a greyish, hybrid hard-paste. The Imari pattern and the knop are unique to Coalport, while the acanthus-scroll handles and the six-lobed plate are typical.

Coalport made a number of *trompe l'oeil* dishes, continuing a fashion established on the Continent. Here the slight indentations on the rim form Coalport's characteristic six lobes.

This ice pail was made at Coalport early in the 19thC. The decoration was set against a solid dark blue

D-shaped crocus pots are rarely marked, so attribution can be a problem, but these have been confirmed as Coalport: similar pots were signed by Baxter who painted Coalport blanks.

135

MINTON

*A pâte-sur-pâte vase, by Marc-Louis Solon
c.1875; ht 15in/38cm; value code D/E.*

Identification checklist for Minton porcelain
1. If the piece is soft-paste, is it thinly potted with a greyish glaze?
2. If the piece is hard-paste, is it flawless and is the glaze very smooth?
3. If a figure, is it heavy for its size?
4. Is the decoration on the soft-paste Neo-classical?
5. Is the decoration on the hard-paste Neo-rococo?
6. If the piece is a figure, is it very elaborately decorated and more highly coloured than other English figures?
7. Is the base of the figure heavily modelled with stiff Rococo scrolls? (See *opposite*)
8. Does the piece have a pattern number and a date cipher?

Minton (1798-present)
Minton was founded in 1798 by Thomas Minton, who is said to have invented the "Willow Pattern". The factory has always maintained a consistently high quality and has been one of the most innovative in Britain.

Paste and glaze
The early soft-paste, from 1798 to c.1810, is thinly potted with a slightly greyish glaze and sometimes has fine black specks in it, especially on the base. The later hard-paste, after 1821, is among the finest and cleanest of

all British porcelains. It is rarely flawed, and the glaze is thin and glassy and extremely smooth, particularly compared to the more musliny glaze on the soft-paste.

Wares

Early soft-paste wares were painted or printed with Neo-classical designs. Later hard-paste wares were usually copied from 18thC Sèvres or Meissen, with moulded borders and pierced rims.

This is an excellent example of the fine, pierced basketweave borders made at Minton in the late 19thC. The centre is painted in a sentimental style typical of several other contemporary factories, but few could match the quality of the basketweave.

Decorative wares

Minton's decorative wares included flower-encrusted objects similar to those made at Coalbrookdale and Rockingham. But, like Coalport, the factory also made Sèvres- style vases and jars with coloured grounds.
* In 1870 the modeller Marc-Louis Solon arrived from Sèvres and introduced the *pâte-sur-pâte* technique, whereby white slip was built up and carved on a dark coloured ground, such as pink, green or blue. The painstaking process often took several weeks to complete and was extremely costly, but the effect could be stunning.

Figures

The early Minton figures were mostly romantic shepherds and shepherdesses in 18thC costume. These were either elaborately decorated with flowered clothes or else left in the biscuit.
* Other subjects included foreign costumes and famous characters, such as theatrical personalities.

* In the late 1840s Minton began to model figures in Parian, a type of porcelain which looks like marble. Most Parian figures are portrait busts or statuettes of romantic maidens.

As well as figures, Minton made a large number of candlestick groups. This example was modelled c.1835.
* The heavily modelled Rococo scrolls on the base are typical of the figures as well as the candlesticks.
* The detailed features and the dense flowers on the costumes are characteristic of Minton. Faces are usually highly coloured. Although Derby and other factories made similar figures, their decoration is usually simpler.

The *pâte-sur-pâte* technique was continued well into the 20thC, but, although the quality was still very high, the pieces lacked the vitality of the 19thC examples.
* These plates, made c.1918, have the pseudo-Chinese pierced and square-scrolled borders which were then very popular at Minton.

Marks

The earliest mark was based on the interlaced "Ls" of Sèvres.
* The mid-19thC mark was an impressed "Minton", and after 1863 "Mintons".
* Until c.1900 alchemical-style date ciphers were also impressed.
* Pattern numbers were also used.

SPODE

*A Spode bone china ornithological dessert service
1815-20; value code D/E*

Identification checklist for Spode porcelain
1. Is the piece made of bone china?
2. Is the bone china pure white in appearance?
3. Is the piece very thinly potted?
4. If the piece is part of a service, is it moulded in relief?
5. Is the decoration an Imari pattern?
6. Is the ground colour lavender-blue?
7. Is the gilding of a high quality?
8. Is the piece marked with a pattern number in red?

Spode (1776-present)
The Spode factory at Stoke-on-Trent in Staffordshire was founded by Josiah Spode in 1776. By 1800 it had developed probably the first formula for English bone china. In 1813 the founder's son, Josiah II, went into partnership with W. T. Copeland, and in 1833 he was bought out by Copeland and T. Garrett. The factory is still in operation and is now merged with Worcester.

Paste and glaze
The paste is pure white, close grained and as smooth as icing (confectioner's) sugar. The glaze is thin, very smooth and white.

Wares
The majority of Spode porcelain was table wares and ornamental wares, which until about 1850 were almost all derived from Roman or Etruscan forms.

Decoration
The factory used various printing techniques, and in the early years it specialized in bat printing – using bats of soft glue instead of paper transfers to produce monochrome vignettes of landscapes and Neo-classical scenes.
* Decorative wares were more ambitiously painted with densely packed botanical subjects, topographical views and copies of Old Master paintings.
* Like Derby, Spode produced a wide range of Imari patterns, but the Spode versions were much more meticulously painted.

Figures
The Spode-Copeland factory was the first to develop Parian, a form of porcelain simulating marble. From 1844 onwards it produced a wide range of Parian figures and busts after the leading sculptors of the day. Almost every piece was marked with the sculptor's name.

made at Worcester, Derby and Coalport, but even without its pattern number and its painted mark this one could easily be identified as Spode by the exceptionally pure white of its ground colour.

This Etruscan vase, made c.1810-20, is described in the pattern book as a "beaded new-shape jar". The applied beads around the rim and the foot, which Spode continued to use until c.1830, are borrowed from the simulated jewels on late 18thC Sèvres.
* The large painted flowers on a gilt-scale and solid (blue) ground are one of the best-known and most elaborate patterns.

This service has several features typical of the fine wares made by Spode in the first quarter of the 19thC:-
* delicate raised white patterns on the borders
* butterfly handles on the sauce tureens
* precise, large-scale botanical painting.

Spode produced a considerable number of tall, bucket-shaped spill vases, which were mostly either plain or decorated with the typical borders of applied beads.

This Parian group of *The sleep of sorrow and the dream of joy* was modelled after an original by Rafaelle Monti in about 1875.
* Portrait busts of statesmen and large-scale models of scantily-clad maidens were among the most popular Parian subjects.

Marks

Before 1830 the most common mark was a hand-painted "SPODE". By 1820 the mark was also being printed. After 1833 "COPELAND & GARRETT" was written in a circle with "LATE SPODE" in the middle.
* Pattern numbers are usually painted in red.

This Imari-pattern plate was made c.1825. Similar plates were

NANTGARW AND SWANSEA

A Swansea ice pail
1814-22; ht 8in/20cm; value code D

Identification checklist for Nantgarw and Swansea
1. Is the paste pure white?
2. Is the glaze smooth and glassy and virtually flawless?
3. Is the piece either pure white or duck-egg blue by transmitted light?
4. Are there three spurs arranged in a triangle of small iridescent circles on the base?
5. If the piece is a plate, is the border moulded in shallow relief with Rococo cartouches?
6. Is the flower decoration of a very high quality?
7. Is the mark right? (see *opposite*)

Nantgarw and Swansea (1813-22)

Probably the finest porcelain made in Britain in the early 19thC came from South Wales. Hoping to rival the quality of French porcelain, the great Derby decorator William Billingsley set up a factory at Nantgarw in 1813 with financial support from William Weston Young. Their porcelain was the most difficult of all to fire. Up to 90 per cent was lost in the kiln. After only a year they moved to Swansea to join forces with Lewis Weston Dillwyn's Cambrian Pottery. Dillwyn experimented with several new formulae, but in 1817, when he withdrew from the business, Billingsley and Young returned to reopen the Nantgarw factory. Although Billingsley left in 1820 to take up a job at Coalport, Young managed to keep the business running for another two years, with Thomas Pardoe, a china painter from Bristol, acting as chief decorator.

Wares

Most Welsh porcelain consists of tea wares or flat wares – dishes and plates – which were fired on spurs in a triangular arrangement of small iridescent circles. Large hollow wares, such as ice pails, are extremely rare: many services had to be supplemented from other factories such as Paris.

Paste and glaze

Nantgarw porcelain is often heavier than Swansea's. It is very translucent and almost pure white when held up to a light. Nantgarw glaze is thick and smooth, with none of the rippling found on the later and thinner Swansea wares.
* Swansea has at least three different types of porcelain, almost all extant examples of which are virtually flawless:
1. duck egg, which is extremely thinly potted and has a decidedly green tone in transmitted light
2. the trident, named after its impressed mark, which is smooth bodied but still quite heavily potted
3. the so-called glassy variety, which is very similar to contemporary Paris porcelain, with which it is often confused.

Decoration

Swansea wares were decorated by some of the best ceramic artists and gilders in Britain, including Thomas Baxter, William Pollard, Henry Morris and Billingsley himself. The quality of their flower painting in particular had few equals.
* Many of the wares from Swansea and Nantgarw were decorated by independent workshops in London.

This butter tub is from a service reputed to have been made at Nantgarw for the Duke of Gloucester when he married his cousin, Princess Mary, in 1816. Based on a Sèvres pattern of 1770, it has a solid coloured ground, which is rare for the Welsh factories, but the delicate, pink-dominated flower painting is typical.

Marks

The Nantgarw mark, impressed in roman letters, is "NANT-GARW CW" (the "CW" stands for china works).
* Swansea marks are either impressed or stencilled, usually in red enamel.
* There are some extremely dubious script Swansea marks around, often on plates which were actually made in Paris.

The Sèvres influence can also be seen on this London-decorated Nantgarw plate, which has been painted with an exotic bird in the style of the famous service made for the MacIntosh family.
* Most of the Nantgarw wares which were decorated in London have a faint border of iridescence around the painting, probably caused by a combination of the different enamel mixtures and the different firing techniques.

This miniature candlestick is very typical of the small pieces made at Swansea. Wild flowers and fruit, particularly wild strawberries, dog roses and speedwells were a particular speciality of the decorators.

This oblong meat dish, decorated by Henry Morris, comes from the Lysaght service, one of the most famous services produced by the Swansea factory. Morris had a neat and somewhat academic style, whereas the other great Swansea decorator, William Pollard, was more "romantic" and expansive. Pollard's plates often have loose cuttings spread around the rim.

141

VAUXHALL

A Chinese-form Vauxhall bottle decorated in deutsche Blumen
c.1755; ht 7½in/19cm; value code C/D

Identification checklist for Vauxhall porcelain
1. Is the porcelain soft-paste?
2. Has the unglazed porcelain burned brown in the firing?
3. Is the decoration a Chinoiserie design with islands, pavillions and pine trees or a bouquet of Meissen-style flowers painted in a lively palette?
4. Is the piece under 8in/20cm high?
5. If the piece is blue and white, is the blue inky or wet-looking? Vauxhall blue is often called "sticky blue".
6. Is the glaze on the blue and white ware patchy, with a strong greenish or bluish tone?
7. Does the porcelain body show small rips or tears under the glaze?

Vauxhall (c.1753-64)
After Chelsea and Bow, the most important of the London porcelain factories was the small Vauxhall China Works, which was set up beside the old-established Lambeth delft potteries by Nicholas Crisp in 1753. After the factory closed in 1764, Crisp made an ill-fated attempt to found a second factory at Bovey Tracey in Devon, where he died in 1774.

Wares

The factory made mostly tea wares, goat and bee jugs similar to those at Chelsea and Derby, candlesticks, *jardinières*, snuff boxes and over 20 different forms of sauceboat.
* Shapes were based on delftware, stoneware, silver and, like the bladder-shaped vase in the main picture, Chinese export wares.

Decoration

Under the influence of the Delft potteries, most Vauxhall wares were decorated in Chinoiserie designs in an inky and wet-looking underglaze blue. But the factory also used bright polychrome enamels, not only for Chinoiserie designs but for tentative, Meissen-style flowers, like those in the main picture.
* The factory also produced a number of armorial wares and pieces decorated with transfer prints of military heroes, such as the Duke of Marlborough, Admiral Howe and the King of Prussia.

Figures

Vauxhall figures are rare. Bases are in Rococo style, often with unusually large flower heads. A set of Four Seasons was made and impressed with the letter K. A figure modeller from Vauxhall joined the Plymouth factory so there are similarities between some Plymouth and Vauxhall figures.

Paste and glaze

The Vauxhall factory used a softpaste. During firing, unglazed areas discoloured brown and the larger pieces, such as the vase in the main picture, tended to sag a bit.
* On polychrome wares the glaze is creamy and opaque, but on blue and white wares it has a bluish or greenish colour which becomes quite deep where it has pooled.

The base, *above*, of the beaker, *bottom left*, shows the discolouring in unglazed areas and the spurious Chinese marks often used at Vauxhall.
* Crude trimming also identifies the piece as Vauxhall rather than Worcester or Liverpool.

On this bottle vase, the bright palette has been used to paint the sort of Chinoiserie design which is more usually found on blue and white London delftware.
* The slight sagging caused by firing is particularly noticeable.

Limehouse (c.1745-48)

Although the least known of the London factories, the little Limehouse factory was one of the pioneers of English porcelain manufacture. It was probably the first English factory to make blue and white porcelain; and many wares previously ascribed to the Liverpool factories of William Reid and William Ball are now known to have been made at Limehouse. The output included:
* shell-shaped dishes
* wavy-edged sauceboats with tripod feet shaped like lions' heads or cherubs
* teapots in a variety of shapes
* Chinoiserie pickle dishes.
The earliest wares seem to have a pinkish tinge, but the later glaze is like a tin glaze, making them resemble Chinese export wares.

This Chinese-shaped beaker is decorated in a style often associated with Liverpool porcelain or London delftware, but the inky blue and the irregular, smudged effect of the glaze are typical of Vauxhall.

LONGTON HALL

A Longton Hall potpourri vase
1775; ht 16in/40.6cm; value code E/F

Identification checklist for Longton Hall porcelain
1. Is the porcelain soft-paste?
2. Is the piece heavily constructed?
3. Does it have firing cracks?
4. Has it collapsed slightly?
5. If a hollow figure, has it a smooth interior?
6. Is the surface of the piece greenish or greyish?
7. Is the glaze peppered with tiny black pin-holes?
8. Are there broad washes of dark, runny underglaze blue?
9. Are tureens or plates moulded in the form of a leaf or a vegetable?
10. Are the veins on the leaves detailed in puce?
11. Is the mark right? (see *opposite*)

Longton Hall (1740-60)

The first of the famous Staffordshire factories was founded at Longton Hall in 1749 by a saltglaze manufacturer, William Littler. During its short life, it made eccentric and slightly primitive wares and figures, often in shapes which showed the influence of saltglaze stoneware.

Wares and figures

The factory made mostly blue and white utilitarian wares, lively copies of Chinese *famille rose* patterns and a famous range of fruit- and vegetable-shaped tureens and jugs, similar to those made at Chelsea and Worcester.
* The first figures were heavily glazed and poorly defined white models of humans and animals which have become known as "the snowman family". Later figures were slightly clumsy copies of Bow, Derby or Meissen.

Paste and glaze

Longton Hall porcelain is a heavy soft-paste, rather like Chelsea's, with a surface that is often slightly irregular.
* The greyish glaze, containing tin, has been described by the great authority W.B. Honey as resembling paraffin wax.

Palette

The Longton Hall palette is unlike any other factory's and again shows the influence of saltglaze wares. The most characteristic colours are:
* yellowish lime green
* crimson puce
* deep underglaze "Littler's Blue".

This barrel-shaped tankard with a fine ridged footrim dates from 1755-6 and is a typical Longton Hall pattern.
* The ear-shaped handle with its double projections on the lower third is much more complicated than most mid-18thC handles.

In 1760, financial problems forced Littler to close Longton Hall and sell out to William Duesbury of Derby. Littler moved to West Pans in Scotland, where he started another factory (1764-77). West Pans porcelain returned to the early paste and glaze used at Longton in the early 1750s, as illustrated in the dish *above*. Almost all West Pans wares include decoration in "Littler's Blue", the distinctive, deep and rather runny underglaze invented by Littler and used at both of his factories.

This moulded dish was made c.1755 to a pattern unknown at any other factory. The beautifully painted sprays of flowers are one of the reasons why Longton Hall wares are sometimes thought to have been made at Derby.
* The dish was decorated by an identifiable but unknown artist, who has since become known as "the trembly rose painter".

Both Longton Hall and Derby made very similar figures of *Summer* and *Autumn*. But the two versions are not difficult to tell apart: on these Longton Hall examples, which were made around 1756, the slightly stiff postures and the doll-like faces are much too simple to be Derby. The fine, delicate sprays of flowers on the clothes and the scrolled bases with frills, particularly on the girl, are also more characteristic of Longton Hall than of Derby.

Marks

The Longton Hall mark consists of two reversed "L"s – standing for Littler and Longton – occasionally accompanied by one or more dots. On some pieces, these look slightly like the crossed swords of Meissen.
* Although it is sometimes possible to find genuine pieces on which the Longton Hall mark has been impressed, it is far more likely to be painted in underglaze blue.

Longton Hall is especially noted for slightly awkward *trompe l'oeil* fruit and vegetable tureens.
* Although other factories made similar tureens, they did not give them spreading, leaf-shaped feet.
* Puce veining and pale edges on the leaves are also typical.

ROCKINGHAM

A Rockingham ice pail from the William IV Dessert Service
c.1830-37; ht 15in/38cm: value code C/D

Identification checklist for Rockingham porcelain
1. Is the porcelain hard-paste and ivory coloured?
2. Does the glaze have very fine crazing?
3. If the piece is a plate, does it have a "C" scroll border?
4. Has the colour sunk into the glaze?
5. Is the modelling of a much lower standard than the paste, the glaze, the palette and the gilding?
6. Is the mark right (see *opposite*)?
7. If the piece is part of a service, does it have a pattern number either lower than 1559 or, if fractional, between 2/1 and 2/78?

Rockingham (1826-42)

In 1826, with the help of the considerable financial backing provided by their landlord, Earl Fitzwilliam, the Brameld family opened a porcelain factory at Swinton in Yorkshire and named it after the Marquis of Rockingham, from whom the earl had inherited his estate. Ignoring utilitarian pieces, they concentrated on ambitious products which were so sumptuous that they were seldom profitable. One of their most

famous projects, the William IV Dessert Service, took seven years to make. In the end the pursuit of excellence ruined them, and the insolvent factory was forced to close in 1842.

Paste and glaze

Rockingham porcelain is a warm, ivory-toned and very high quality hard-paste.

The glaze is sometimes blemished by crazing, which can be so fine that it is invisible to the naked eye.

Neo-rococo

Although Rockingham made a number of pieces in the Neo-classical style, it is best known for being at the forefront of the Neo-rococo revival. However, Rockingham wares are rare: many of the elaborately moulded and flower encrusted wares which are still attributed to the factory were in fact made by the other English factories which followed its example. The most common Rockingham products are figures and small-scale decorative wares, particularly:-
* violeteers (see *below*)
* *potpourri* vases.

Many factories produced teapots of this shape in the 1830s and 40s, but there are a number of elaborate embellishments which can identify a pot as Rockingham:-
* a crown knop
* projecting spurs on the handle.
* a cover recessed beneath flared sides
* a spout sharply moulded with acanthus leaves
* pronounced moulded vertical ribs on the bombé sides of the pot
* three rudimentary leaf feet.

This violeteer, which is less than 4½in/11.4cm tall, was made. c.1835 and epitomizes Rockingham's emphasis on modelling and surface decoration. The handles and the spout are made in the form of branches, foreshadowing the naturalism of the 1840s.

Rockingham figures were made only between 1826 and 1830. Although the modelling is not always of the highest standard, the quality of the paste, glaze, palette and gilding make them generally superior to similar figures from Derby and Staffordshire. They are also sparingly decorated, and the colours are not so harsh.

Marks

From 1826 to 30 the standard mark is the griffin from the Fitzwilliam crest over the words "Rockingham Works Brameld".
* A rarer version has "Rockingham Works" above the griffin and "Brameld" underneath.
* After 1830 "Manufacturer to the King" was usually added. Rare versions for this period include "Royal Rockingham Brameld".
* On figures, the mark is usually impressed rather than printed.

Rockingham made a variety of Neo-rococo plates with moulded "C" scrolled borders. This one was decorated c.1830 by William Bailey, one of the factory's most accomplished artists. Similar plates were made at Spode and Coalport, but at these factories the scrolls were used to enclose reserves and not just as borders.
* In general Rockingham's Neo-rococo was less extreme than Coalport's.

147

DERBY WARES

A Derby botanical dessert service
1795-1800; value code A/B

Identification checklist for Derby wares
1. Is the porcelain soft-paste?
2. Is the paste fine-grained and greyish? (pre-1770)
3. Is the paste pure white? (post-1770)
4. Is the glaze greyish or slightly green? (pre-1770)
5. Is the glaze brilliant? (post-1770)
6. Is the gilding excellent?
7. Are there three patch marks in a triangle on the base? (post-1756)

Derby (1750-1848)
The Derby factory was founded in 1750 by a Frenchman, André Planché. In 1756, it was bought out by John Heath and his partner William Duesbury, who had until then been decorating pieces for Chelsea. In 1770, they also bought the Chelsea factory, and for the next 14 years, in a phase known as Chelsea-Derby, the two concerns operated together. In 1811, the business was acquired from Heath and Duesbury's successors by Robert Bloor, who, despite the fact that he went mad in 1826, continued to manage the declining factory until it closed in 1848. Several other factories were established in Derby in the 19thC. The most successful was the so-called "Crown Derby" company, which survives today as the Royal Crown Derby Porcelain Company.

Paste and glaze
The earliest Derby soft-paste is fine-grained and greyish and has almost the appearance of hard-paste, even in cochouidal fractures.
* The early glaze is greyish white, or sometimes greyish green. Often, there are tiny pin-prick flecks in it.
* Pieces made after the arrival of Duesbury in 1756 have a more refined appearance. Although the paste is still the same, the glaze, which can still be slightly green, is much thinner and more translucent.
* After the acquisition of the Chelsea factory in 1770, the paste and glaze improved to become some of the best in England. The porcelain which Derby made in the last years of the 18thC is pure and quite white, and the glaze is brilliant and often slightly bluish.

Wares

At first almost all the Derby products were figures. Until the introduction of a new formula in 1770, the porcelain tended to split on exposure to boiling water. As a result early tea and coffee wares are extremely rare.

* After 1756, all products were fired on pads of clay, which left a triangle of three greyish patch marks on their bases.

* The majority of early wares were left in the white, and the remainder were decorated in very pale enamel. After 1756 the colours became brighter and clearer.

Underglaze blue

The very rare blue and white wares from Derby are invariably decorated with Chinoiserie and cell diaper, or trellis borders in a slight grey underglaze cobalt.

Designs

After 1770, the quality of design at Derby improved considerably. The leading landscape painters at the factory during this period were Zachariah Boreman and George Robertson. The leading botanical painters were William ("Quaker") Pegg and William Billingsley, both of whom are thought to have worked on the dessert service in the main picture. The Derby gilders inherited Chelsea's mantle as the best in Britain, and often demonstrated their skill by gilding each piece in a service with a different border. Gilders are identified by a number.

* In the 1770s, Derby became the first English factory to introduce pattern numbers. This coffee pot *below*, c.1756-48, is a rare example of early Derby tea and coffee wares. The acanthus leaf

moulding on the spout and the ribbing are typical. Although other factories, including Chelsea and Worcester, made vessels with moulded ribbing, they did not end it so far from the rim.

* The figures are like Worcester's but Derby's palette included a distinctive opaque turquoise. This small circular Derby basket *below*, made around 1760, is known as a "spectacle" basket because the

pierced parts of the sides are shaped like spectacles. The shape is not known at any other factory.

* The exotic birds are very typical, loosely painted copies of Chelsea red-anchor designs, which were in turn copied from Sèvres. But by the time this was painted, Chelsea was making sumptuous gold-anchor wares with copious gilding.

* The "rope-twist" handles and the applied flowers at terminals and intersections were used by several factories, but Derby tended to use two colours instead of one to decorate the handles, and its flowers are on a slightly larger scale, with centres that look like hollow tubes.

* These three plates *below* are typical of Derby between 1780 and

1800. The "Named View" plate on the left, from the famous Chatsworth service, has a typically small Neo-classical landscape panel.

* The plate in the centre is decorated with a puce Rococo cameo of *putti*, in the manner of Sèvres.

* Monochrome cameos of *putti*, like the one on the *right*, were common, but the fine gilt border identifies the plate as Derby.

Isleworth c.1766-1800

A small number of "Derby" underglaze blue wares have been re-attributed to Isleworth following a dig on site in 1997. It made tea and dinner wares in blue pattern and printed designs, similar to Derby and Lowestoft wares of the period.

DERBY FIGURES

A pair of Derby figures of Europa and the Bull *and* Leda and the Swan
c.1765; ht 11in/28cm; value code E

Identification checklist for Derby figures
1. Is the figure dry-edged? (see *opposite*)
2. Is it decorated in a subdued palette in which turquoise, pink and iron-red predominate? (pre-1811)
3. Is the figure over-decorated? (post-1811)
4. Is the base integrated with the figure?
5. Are the paste and the glaze right? (see *previous page*)
6. Is the mark right? (see *opposite*)
7. Are there patch-marks on the base (see p. 149)?

Early figures

It has been suggested that Duesbury encouraged Planché (see pp.148-9) to make figures because he could not get enough from Chelsea for his workshops to decorate. However, the earliest Derby figures are of a much lower standard than the Chelsea products. Representing the usual range of pastoral and allegorical subjects, they are stifly modelled – although this may be due to the overplasticity of the clay – and they stand on simple mound bases, similar to those on the early Meissen figures of Kändler. Fortunately, most of them have been left in the white. The few that have been decorated are very primitive. For example, the mouths are often so badly painted that the lips look over-large and misshapen.

This figure of a "gallant" has the typical "wooden" posture of early Derby. The simple attempt at a Rococo scroll on the base shows

that the piece was made around 1755, shortly before Duesbury took over, when the factory was becoming more sophisticated.
* Before 1756, the glutinous glaze was wiped away from the edge of the base to prevent it from sticking the figure to the supports in the kiln during the firing. As a result, the figures from this period are known as "Dry-edge Derby".

Early Duesbury-period figures
In the early years of Duesbury's management, the modellers at Derby were still constrained by the weakness of the clay, but their figures are much livelier and have a greater subtlety and grace. Many of them look as though they have just got up from a comfortable chair and are stretching their long limbs. Like the mythological pair in the main picture, they stand on elaborate bases which integrate completely with the figures, quite unlike the products of any other English factory. Their clothes are covered in neat, delicate, lightly painted flowers, and they are decorated in a fairly subdued palette in which the dominant colours are usually turquoise, pink and iron-red.

In the last quarter of the 18thC, when taste changed from the Rococo to Neo-classicism, Derby followed the example of many European factories and produced some fine biscuit figures. Modelled by Pierre Stephan, William Coffee and J. J. Spengler, the son of the director of the Zürich factory, these elegant and detailed figures are among the best products of Derby, and are seriously undervalued today. On this group, the *Graces adoring Pan*, which was modelled by Pierre

Stephan around 1775, the crisp modelling of the faces and the drapery is unobscured by heavy glaze.
* The influence of Tournai and other Continental factories is evident in the architectural nature of the rockwork and the circular order of the figures.

The contrast between the Rococo and Neo-classical styles at Derby is highlighted dramatically in these two figures. The large figure, *above, left*, represents the famous actor James Quin in the role of Falstaff. With its large flowers and bright combination of turquoise, pink and iron red, the figure could only be Derby or Chelsea, but the three patch marks on the base identify it as Derby. The Neo-classical figure of Shakespeare, *above, right*, made around 1790, has a simple chamfered rectangular base and is much more restrained in its colouring.

Bloor
Under Bloor (see p. 148) the quality of the figures declined. Most were overdecorated, with heavily rouged cheeks, sombre colours and square, octagonal or even debased Rococo bases.

Marks
Derby wares and figures were not marked until the acquisition of Chelsea in 1770. From 1770 to 84 various combinations of the anchor and the letter "D" were used, usually in gilding. However, the commonest mark is a crown over a "D". From 1782 until 1825, the mark was a crown over crossed batons and a "D" with three dots either side of the batons. Before 1806 the usual colours were puce or blue. After that red was used exclusively.

VENICE

A Vezzi teapot
1723-27; ht 5 ⁷/₈ in/15cm; value code A

Identification checklist for Venetian porcelain
Vezzi
1. Is the piece heavily potted?
2. Is the decoration applied or moulded?
3. Is there a noticeable wreathing in the body?
4. Is the glaze brownish where it has pooled?
Cozzi
1. Does the piece look greyish?
2. Is it marked with a clumsy red anchor?
3. Do the handles or the spouts look eccentric?
4. Is the palette dominated by a combination of iron-red, puce and iridescent green?

Vezzi (1720-27)
The third European factory to make hard-paste porcelain was founded in Venice by two goldsmiths, Francesco Vezzi and Christoph Conrad Hunger, who stole the formula from his former employer, at Meissen. The firm closed in 1735 and only a few pieces have survived.

Vezzi paste and glaze
The Vezzi paste is very similar to Vienna's, which was also acquired through Hunger. Highly translucent, and varying in colour from dead white through ivory to slightly grey, it is usually very thickly potted and can look quite lumpy and uneven. On turned pieces, such as bowls and teapots, there is a noticeable "wreathing" in the body, as on Champion's Bristol.

The glaze is clear and has a surface like melted ice, but it is occasionally suffused with tiny bubbles, and it sometimes gathers in brownish areas, as can be seen on the teapot *above*.

Shapes
Like all the early Baroque factories, Vezzi relied on Chinese forms or heavy silver shapes, like the one used on the teapot in the main picture.

Decoration
Most Vezzi wares are moulded in shallow relief, either with festoons, swags and flowers, or else with stiff, Böttger-type leaves (such as those on the teapot), gadroons, or a debased *blanc-de-Chine* relief work.
* Coloured decoration are in both enamels and underglaze blue.
* The palette is similar to early Meissen or du Paquier, but the painting is often a bit primitive.
* Designs are usually Chinoiserie or floral patterns, or large-scale classical and *Commedia dell'Arte* subjects by Ludovico Ortolani.

Decoration
Applied flowers are common on Cozzi wares, but the usual form of decoration is painting, in which iron-red, puce and a luscious irridescent green predominate.
* The most common decorative design are:
1. flowers, which are quite detailed on early pieces
2. unframed landscapes with fanciful buildings
3. simple Chinoiserie
4. classical figures, contained in scrollwork or solid borders.

Cozzi figures
Cozzi produced a large range of figures, including corpulent Meissen-style pagoda figures, *Commedia dell'Arte* characters, dwarves modelled after the engravings of Jacques Callot and pyramid-shaped groups.

With their compressed globular shapes, the teapot and sucrier in this tea service, made c.1725, are similar to early Meissen or Vienna wares, but the straight-sided "U"-shape with a relatively wide footrim on the two tea bowls and the deep saucer are unique to Vezzi.

Coffee cans and saucers were among the most popular of Cozzi's wares. These examples, made c.1770, have a typical combination of eccentric Chinoiserie and a semi-Neo-classical wreath border. The ear-shaped and apparently melting handle is unique to Cozzi.

Marks
The Vezzi mark is "Venezia", or an abbreviation, such as "Ven:a" incised or painted in underglaze blue, blue, red or gold. However, some pieces are unmarked.

Cozzi (1764-1812)
The most successful Venetian factory was opened in by Geminiano Cozzi.

Paste and glaze
The paste is greyish and is covered in a thin watery glaze. However, the greyness is not as intense as at Doccia.

Shapes
The shapes generally follow the fashions of contemporary German and French porcelain, but the vessels usually have distinctive handles and spouts.

The over-enthusiastically applied cobalt on this unique documentary vase, dated 1769, is typical of the Cozzi factory.

Cozzi marks
The usual mark is a clumsily drawn anchor in iron-red, but it cannot be confused with Chelsea, which is smaller and much neater.

Other factories
The other two Venice factories are Hewelke, established in 1758, and Le Nove, which opened in 1752.

CAPODIMONTE AND BUEN RETIRO

A Capodimonte Commedia dell'Arte *group by G.Ricci
c.1750; ht 6½in/16.5cm; value code A*

Identification checklist for Capodimonte porcelain
1. Is the porcelain pure white?
2. Is it translucent and very refined, like icing (confectioner's) sugar?
3. Is the glaze lustrous?
4. If a tea and coffee ware, is it very thinly potted?
5. Is the decoration stippled or drawn with extremely fine brushwork?
6. If a figure, is it pyramidal?
7. Are flesh tones rendered in a violet colour?
8. Does the base have an unglazed margin running around the bottom?

Capodimonte (1743-59)
The most famous Italian porcelain factory was founded by Charles III of Bourbon, King of Naples, who established it in the grounds of his palace at Capodimonte.

Buen Retiro (1760-1808)
When Charles III became king of Spain in 1759 he took the entire staff of his factory with him to Madrid, and in the following year opened a new factory in the palace of Buen Retiro. This factory concentrated on figures and was active until 1808. However, the quality of the fine soft-paste deteriorated towards the end of the 18thC, and in 1803 a hard-paste was introduced.

Paste and glaze
Capodimonte produced some of the most liquidly beautiful of all soft-paste porcelain. The paste is close-grained and very white, not unlike the *blanc-de-Chine* ware from Dehua in southern China. The porcelain is covered in a brilliant glaze with the merest hint of an ivory tone, which makes it look very like St Cloud wares.

Wares
The factory began by basing its wares on Meissen or Chinese wares, with moulded shapes and carefully-painted floral designs. These pieces tend to be very thinly potted, in contrast to their French counterparts.

This teacup and saucer, made c.1750, are painted in the early, pale, soft-focused Capodimonte palette. Like many wares of this period, they are decorated with Chinoiserie scenes. The fine brush strokes and stippled, almost pointilliste technique are typical, as is the delicate, somewhat outdated gilding.

Capodimonte made a large number of shell-moulded snuff boxes. The insides of the lids were usually decorated with battles, marine subjects or classical scenes, as on this example, made c.1745-50, and, as here, figures were often set against a grey-toned landscape and highlighted in blue and puce. The subtle colouring of the shells is characteristic of these early wares.

These lovers, *below*, c.1745-50, have the violet-toned flesh of all Capodimonte figures. Although painted in the early pastel palette, they are unusually fully coloured. Untypically, Gricci has given them naturally proportioned heads – most of his figures had disproportionately small heads, like those on p. 154.

The influence of Meissen is clearly evident on this coffee pot, which was made in 1755. The scattered flowers and insects are loosely based on the work of Klinger. However, the delicate gilding and the angular scrolled handle are typically Capodimonte.

Figures

Capodimonte figures are among the finest soft-paste figures ever made, and Gricci ranks among the greatest modellers. Despite the shortcomings of soft-paste, the figures show a high degree of liveliness and delicacy. Most are set on rockwork, mound or simple slab bases, with unglazed margins around the sides where the excess glaze has been wiped away before firing. The uneven glaze is usually obvious on the underside.

Marks

The usual mark, at both factories is a *fleur-de-lys*, impressed, painted in gold, or crudely drawn in underglaze blue.

DOCCIA

A Doccia tea and coffee service
c.1750; value code C

Identification checklist for Doccia porcelain
1. Does the porcelain appear grey?
2. If the piece is a ware, is it moulded with relief figures?
3. If a large scale ware, has it split in the firing?
4. Are wares decorated with transfer printing in underglaze blue, or with stencilling?
5. If the piece is a coloured figure with a scroll base, is the base vigorously moulded and detailed in puce?
6. Do figures and moulded decorations have unnaturally reddish flesh tones?
7. Is the mark convincing? (see *opposite*)

Doccia (1735-present)
The Doccia factory was founded by the Marchese Carlo Ginori in 1735 and is still operating today.

Paste and glaze
The early porcelain at Doccia was a type of greyish hard-paste. The characteristically thin glaze of Doccia porcelain emphasizes the underlying greyness, making

it easy to recognize. However, the tone can be confused with Vezzi porcelain (see pp. 152-3), notably on pieces made during the first years, when Doccia had no mark.

Palette
In the 18th and early 19thC, the most prominent colours were puce and iron-red, followed by sky-blue, yellow and green.

Wares

The majority of the factory's output has always been wares, particularly tea and dinner services and small useful and decorative wares, such as boxes and caskets.

Decoration

One of the most popular forms of decoration on Doccia wares is the shallow relief moulding of classical subjects. As on the service on the previous page, the design is often quite crowded, and the figures are detailed in rather strong flesh colours.

* Two of the best known Doccia patterns are *à tulipano*, an Oriental spray of red peonies, and *à galletto*, red and gold Chinese cockerels. Compared to these, the Imari copies are slightly crude.
* Other wares were decorated with stencilling, known as *stampino*.
* Doccia was also one of the very few Continental factories to use transfer printing in underglaze blue.

Doccia made a number of high quality armorial wares. This sucrier, made 1745-50, has a quatrelobed, Meissen form and its painting derives from the work of Meissen's leading decorator, J. G. Klinger, but the brilliant green colour and delicate scrollwork are typical of the Anreiter family, who worked at Doccia from 1735-46.

This plate, c.1750, is of contemporary silver form, and similar to French *faïence* wares. Another similarity between the two is the tin glaze with which Doccia covered some of its porcelain from 1750-c.1770. But Doccia also used warm colours and gilding, which was forbidden to all French firms except Sèvres.

The meticulous painting on this small snuffbox, c.1790-1800, is typical of Doccia's best wares. The subject is probably based on architectural prints from the factory's own collection.

Figures

Doccia made numerous slip-cast figures. Many represent classical subjects and are often massively proportioned. They are crisply modelled with well-defined musculature and have usually been left in the white.

* The bases made during the Rococo period are quite vigorously modelled.

In addition to the characteristic bases, these salts from the 1770s have Doccia's typical intensely coloured eyes, mouths and hair.

Miniature busts

Miniature busts were quite popular at Doccia. They are usually less than 4in/10cm high, although they have the same Rococo bases as larger figures.

Marks

The mark, introduced after Carlo Ginori's death in 1757, is a star, either impressed or painted in red, blue or gold.

* A crowned "N" was used on wares which copied Capodimonte. (This mark was used on fakes.)

AMERICAN PORCELAIN

A Union Porcelain Works vase by Karl Muller made for the Philadelphia Centennial in 1876

From their earliest days, American porcelain manufacturers had to struggle against competition from England, Continental Europe and the Far East which the American public usually perceived as superior. This meant that few American ceramics firms enjoyed widespread commercial success, especially during the boom periods of production in Europe. In fact, many factories only survived long enough to lose their initial capital investment.

American porcelain has been virtually ignored by modern collectors, and even the relatively abundant post-Centennial wares made by large, established companies have remained undocumented until recent years. Porcelain from small American factories, most of which is unmarked, provides one of the few challenging areas left to the modern collector.

The history of American porcelain is closely linked to developments in England and France, and in particular to the efforts and skills of immigrant potters. The first recorded pieces were a small group of bowls made by Andrew Duche in Savannah, Georgia, in c.1738, which predate English porcelain by at least six years. Duche's work was almost certainly not commercial and no examples of his porcelain survive, but the raw materials he mined in Virginia and North Carolina were later used by English manufacturers, notably William Cookworthy at Plymouth. The first commercial manufacturer of American porcelain was the American China Manufactury of Bonnin & Morris (see pp.162-3) which survived for only two years. No significant manufacturer of porcelain operated in the United States for over 40 years after Bonnin & Morris's well-publicized failure. But by the 1820s, porcelain in the fashionable French taste was being made and decorated in small factories throughout the North-East. The best known of these firms was Tucker & Partners (see pp.160-61) in Philadelphia, which was in operation from 1825 until 1838. Unlike most earlier American wares, which show the distinct influence of either English or French taste, Tucker porcelains combine European forms and materials with American proportions and motifs.

The heavy immigration from Europe into the United States during the 1840s provided new talents for the potting trade and a greatly expanded domestic market. Porcelain factories were established in Ohio, Vermont, New Jersey and New York City, where there was a concentration of factories in the Greenpoint section of Brooklyn. This group included Charles Cartlidge's Pottery (see pp.164-5). An immigrant from Staffordshire, and a former agent for William Ridgway, who began making porcelain in c.1848, Cartlidge concentrated on decorative hollow wares and an extensive variety of dust-pressed items from buttons to door plaques. Although it closed after eight years, his pottery was the model for a neighbouring factory which operated as the Union Porcelain Works from 1861 until 1910. This factory produced some of the most innovative designs in American porcelain, many of which were the work of European modellers.

The Philadelphia Centennial Exhibition of 1876 gave American porcelain manufacturers a new awareness of the supremacy of overseas competition, particularly from England, France and Japan. But apart from the works established by Ott and Brewer in Trenton, New Jersey in the mid-1860s, few firms could meet the competition on an equal footing. The Ott and Brewer Works used Parian porcelain for high standard sculptural and hollow ware, and in the post-Centennial period it made an ivory coloured porcelain body for expensive decorative wares in the style of Royal Worcester. During the last quarter of the 19thC, Ott and Brewer were also prominent among American manufacturers of extremely thin and intricately formed eggshell porcelain in the style of the Irish Belleek factory. All decorative American eggshell or "eggshell type" porcelain, most of which was made in the Trenton area, is known collectively as American Belleek. The best exponent of American Belleek was the factory established in Trenton in 1889 by Walter Scott Lenox.

WILLIAM ELLIS TUCKER

*A Tucker porcelain pitcher
c.1830; ht approx. 14in/35.5cm; value code D/E*

Identification checklist for William Ellis Tucker porcelain
1. Is the porcelain extremely white and heavy?
2. Is the floral painting of similar style and standard to that found on contemporary English porcelain?
3. Are painted scenes uniquely American?
4. Is the enamel palette comparable to contemporary Paris porcelain?
5. Is the landscape painting comparatively crudely drawn and with a naïve quality?
6. Is the gilding profuse and subject to rubbing?

William Ellis Tucker (1826-38)
Tucker was a wealthy Philadelphian whose factory used clays from Delaware, Pennsylvania, New York and New Jersey as well as refined materials from the failed works of Ducasse and Chanou in New York City. Tucker employed at least two partners, including John Hulme and Joseph Hemphill. After his premature death in 1832, the business was carried on by his younger brother, Thomas Tucker.
* Tucker's factory was the largest American porcelain manufactury in the first half of the 19thC.

Types of wares
Tucker's earliest recorded wares were milk jugs, known in the United States as "china pitchers",

and throughout the factory's history, pitchers of all kinds were among its most successful products. By 1830, Tucker's output included ornamental and spill vases, 12 pitchers, pierced fruit stands, tea wares, a night light, butter dishes, plates, bowls, covered dishes, compotes, and a "spitting box and a funnel".
* Tucker porcelain is not as scarce as pieces by Bonnin & Morris (see pp. 162-3), but it is rarely seen on the market.
* Collectors favour interesting forms and polychrome-decorated examples, especially those with scenes or motifs of American interest, and marked pieces.
* The bodies of Tucker wares are usually very white and glassy.

160

Designs

Most of Tucker's porcelain is French in taste, although English forms were also followed. French models include "Empire" vases and Paris-style useful wares. Most pieces are distinguishable from European wares by their exaggerated proportions.

Decoration

While some of Tucker's products were only sparsely gilded or monogrammed, much of the ware was heavily coated in gilt, which is quite easily rubbed away. The decorative schemes often included simple painted landscapes in sepia or black. Polychrome decoration is limited to floral compositions of variable quality which are notably similar to English Coalport wares, and American scenes or landscapes. Some of these are extremely naïve and may be the work of William Tucker's younger brother Thomas.

No transfer-printed ware is known, and the paste, enamels and gilding closely resemble that used in contemporary Paris.

Marks

Although most Tucker porcelain was unmarked, some pieces carry the maker's name or PHILAD painted in red. The names of Tucker's two known financial partners also occasionally appeared on the marks.

Other makers

Other early 19thC American porcelain makers included the factory of Louis Francois Decasse and Nicolas Louis Edouard Chanou in New York City. They produced heavily gilded Paris-style wares.

This printed mark is found on some of Decasse and Chanou's porcelain made between 1824 and 27.
* Tucker's rival firm of Smith, Fife and Co. was active in c.1830.

Charles Cartlidge (1848-56)

Charles Cartlidge was a potter from Staffordshire who emigrated to New York in 1832. After working as an agent for William Ridgway's English pottery, he set up his own soft-paste factory in Greenpoint, Brooklyn, in 1848. Five years later, when his products had won a prize for quality, he had four large kilns and employed 60 people.

The Cartlidge factory made a large number of moulded pitchers in several sizes. The most common moulded decorations are an oak-leaf motif or corn stalks, such as those on this example, c.1850.
* Other typical wares include "porcelain tea, table and fancy wares", most of which were slip-cast and finished in gilt, or small dust-pressed items, such as buttons.
* Cartlidge paste is similar to contemporary English bone china and is usually thickly potted.
* Most Cartlidge pieces have gilt decoration and monograms are very common.
* Cartlidge porcelain is sometimes marked "American Porcelain" painted in gilt script, but most pieces are unmarked.
* Signed wares and those painted with polychrome American motifs, are very sought-after.

A Bonnin & Morris sweetmeat dish
c.1770; ht 5 5/8 in/13.8cm; value code A

Identification checklist for The American China Manufactory (Bonnin & Morris)
1. Is the item relatively thickly potted?
2. Is the glaze uneven, pitted and bubbled?
3. Are unglazed areas stained a brownish colour?
4. Is the paste "porridgy" and barely translucent?
5. Is moulded ornament, florettes in particular, relatively crudely fashioned?
6. Are painted landscapes unlike those found on contemporary English blue and white porcelain?

The American China Manufactory (1770-72)
This shortlived porcelain firm was founded by Gousse Bonnin and George Anthony Morris in the Southwark district of Philadelphia. It was the first of its kind in the United States but it failed within eighteen months of opening, mainly because neither Bonnin nor Morris had any experience of the ceramics trade, nor access to a successful porcelain formula. Also, they relied on the support of local patrons who baulked at paying up to five times the cost of comparable, imported items. The workforce included nine "master workers" whom Bonnin enticed to Philadelphia from England.
* Bonnin & Morris porcelain is extremely rare and was never exported.

With little justification, the factory consistently compared its wares to the prestigious blue and white porcelain imported into the United States by the English firm of Bow, although the form of this Bow sweetmeat dish may have inspired that of the example on the previous page.

Types of wares

By the spring of 1771 Bonnin & Morris offered a complete range of tablewares, including full tea and dinner services, cups and tea bowls (some moulded with diamond quilting), sauce boats, "dressing boxes", open-work baskets, pickle dishes (of shell and leaf form), and sweetmeat stands. The factory used American clays mixed with calcined animal bones for their porcelain body which is of soft-paste type, and similar to that used at Bow, Lowestoft, Chelsea (gold-anchor) and some Liverpool factories. Most extant pieces are thickly potted but archeological evidence suggests that many were thinly walled. The paste tends to be "porridgy" and may not show translucence except under strong light, when a brownish colour and "moons" are present. Unglazed body areas tend to turn yellowish-brown and the glaze is usually pitted or bubbled, showing pools of a greenish-blue tint.

Decoration

All of the documented pieces by this factory are blue and white, most of them painted in a bold style comparable to that found on contemporary Liverpool porcelain. Painted motifs include conventional diapered borders, Chinoiseries, flowers and landscapes, which sometimes combine English river scenes with Dutch-style buildings. One example exists that is transfer-printed with flowers in the Worcester manner.

Marks

The similarities to English porcelain together with anomalies in even the few documented examples make the search for Bonnin & Morris porcelain and its attribution a daunting endeavour. This is even further confused by the marks. In January 1771, Bonnin & Morris advertised that it would mark all its wares with an "S" (presumably for Southwark), but only one example so marked has ever been found. This was a shard excavated on the factory site.

These are examples of the marks seen on the factory's porcelain, all painted in underglaze blue. Of the 15 or so known pieces, some are unmarked but most carry a "P" (presumably for Philadelphia). One example has four space dots next to the "P". To add to the enigma, at least two pieces are marked with a "Z".

Closure

At the beginning of 1771 Bonnin & Morris appealed to the Assembly in Philadelphia for a loan and ran a lottery in New Castle, Delaware "for the encouragement of the American China Manufactory", but to no avail. By the end of the following year they had closed their factory and were appealing again, this time for charity, on behalf of the now unemployed craftsmen who had been brought over from England. However, the appeal failed and the factory was forced to close for good.

THE UNION PORCELAIN CO.

*A Union Porcelain Heathen-Chinee pitcher
1876; ht 95/8in/23.4cm; value code D/E*

Identification checklist for Union Porcelain (Greenpoint)
1. Is the design highly innovative?
2. Is the modelling comparatively crude?
3. Is the ware thinly potted and brittle?
4. Does the finish appear smear-glazed and the
enamel painting semi-matt?
5. Is the palette pale and muted?
6. Is the gilding poor and subject to rubbing?
7. Are the ornamental motifs exotic and in
extraordinary combinations?

**The Union Porcelain
Company (1861-1910)**
In 1884, William, Anthony and
Francis Victor Boch founded a
pottery on Fifth Street in the
Greenpoint section of Brooklyn.
The Boch brothers' works was
comparable to that operated
by the neighbouring factory of
Charles Cartlidge (see p. 161),
and some moulded pitchers
have been attributed to either. In 1861,
the Boch brothers' firm was
purchased by a managing
partner, Thomas Carl Smith,
who renamed the company the
Union Porcelain Co. (later called
the Union Porcelain Works).

Types of wares
Like Cartlidge, the Boch brothers
made extensive use of Prosser's
dust-pressing patent in the
manufacturing of porcelain
sundries including name plates
and door plaques, but useful
hollow wares were the main
product. For most of its existence,
the Union Porcelain Works was
operated by Charles H.L. Smith,
son of the founder, who expanded
its output in the 1860s to
include decorative table wares,
such as oyster plates. These
were made in a white, glassy
porcelain and usually finished
in lustrous, coloured glazes.

Designs

In the early 1870s Karl Muller, a German-born sculptor, served as art director of the Union Porcelain Works. Muller was responsible for the extraordinary, sculptured designs produced at the works from c.1875, including the famous Century Vase (see p. 158) made for the Philadelphia Centennial exhibition. The vase was made in a small size (12in/30cm), and some examples are signed K. MULLER on the moulded relief portrait of George Washington.

Under Muller's direction, the company's product range expanded to include decorative table wares with exotic moulded ornament such as the "Heathen-Chinee" pitcher, probably designed in 1875, moulded with a figural scene from a contemporary poem. A later version can be seen on p. 164.

Decoration

Muller's repertoire of motifs includes mandarin head-finials, handles shaped like polar bears and other animals, and feet modelled as rabbits. The wares were often decorated with relief-moulded figures, and they were usually painted in a muted palette and extensively gilded. The models of animals are usually realistically coloured. The inspiration for this category of Union Porcelain, which is by far the most collectable and rare, includes Egyptian, Chinese, Japanese and American historical motifs as well as flora and fauna. Many have a Parian-type body with a high or smear glaze.
* As well as being the first American factory to make a true, hard-paste porcelain, the Union Porcelain Works was the first to use underglaze colours.

This Union Porcelain "Liberty cup", modelled by Muller c.1880, ranks with his "Century Vase" among the most famous pieces in the history of American porcelain. Muller trained as a clay sculptor in Paris, and the French influence is particularly evident here in the cup's Neo-rococo foot, the extensive gilding and, of course, the figure of Liberty.

Marks

Few examples of Boch porcelain are marked, although some pitchers moulded with Bacchanalian motifs have an impressed signature. Union Porcelain Works marks include the incised initials "U.P.W." as well as the full factory name painted or stamped and the initials "N.Y." (for New York) or "L.I." (for Long Island).

COPIES AND FAKES

Most porcelain fakes and forgeries were produced in the 20thC, but the business of copying porcelain has an ancient and much more honourable tradition.

During the 18thC the Chinese potters were still following 14thC designs, and inscribing them with earlier, classical reign marks, not with any intention to deceive, but out of respect for the artistry of their predecessors.

In Paris during the late 19thC, the famous Samson factory made many copies of both Oriental and European porcelain, but once again there was seldom any obvious intention to deceive. Most of the pieces carried the factory's "S" mark, and the rest were usually betrayed by other means.

Some of the earliest forgeries, or fraudulent imitations, were the mid-18thC French and English copies which were deceptively inscribed with the prestigious marks of Sèvres and Meissen. Faking, in which pieces were altered to look like something rarer and more valuable, can be said to have started in the late 18thC, when large numbers of Sèvres pieces were bought in the white by independent decorators who painted them in the Sèvres style and inscribed them with its mark.

In the 20thC, when "investment collecting" led to escalating prices, factories were set up all over the Far East to imitate old Oriental wares; some dealers simply removed the "S" from Samson pieces; and in China the finest fakers of all took genuine but mundane Ming pieces, stripped them with acid and redecorated them with rarer designs. Some copies, especially those by Samson, are collectable, particularly larger scale wares, and Imari or *famille rose*-type figures.

American porcelain is seldom copied or faked.

A Samson "famille rose" *chicken tureen*

ORIENTAL PORCELAIN

Early in the 18thC, a few Chinese pieces were imported into Holland in the white and then primitively decorated with harsh colours in both Chinese and Japanese designs; and even a few of the blue and white wares were embellished with additional decorations. But the first convincing forgeries were the rare Tang pieces which flooded the market at the beginning of the 20thC. In the 1920s, dealers began to remove the marks from Samson pieces and pass them off as genuine. And after 1945, when prices rose rapidly, new factories began to make "old" porcelain in China, Japan, Taiwan, Hong Kong, Singapore and Indonesia. At first these forgeries duped several leading dealers – and at least one of the culprits. At a New York sale a Japanese collector bought what he thought was a fine Song-period Longquan vase, only to discover later that it had been made recently in his own factory.

A great deal of Chinese porcelain was decorated in various styles during the 18thC by the Dutch, who often enamelled over the underglaze blue pattern, in a practice known as "clobbering", which gave the pieces a clumsy, overcrowded look. This tankard is a perfect example – a fat cherub has found his way onto a Chinese riverscape.
* "Clobbered" wares may well prove a good investment, as they are poised for reassessment.

This small blue and white wine cup is a copy of an original from the reign of Yongle (1403-24). So far as is known there are only four genuine Yongle wine cups in existence, and the copy was made in 1986 after one of them had realized over half a million dollars at auction. The copyist has caught much of the feeling of the original, but the piece is too heavily potted and the design is much more crowded than it is on the genuine cup.
* Clever forgeries such as this are often betrayed by the poor calligraphy in the reign mark. But in this case, the mark, which is inside the bowl, has been blurred with an abrasive agent. As a result, it looks very like one of the many genuine marks which were distorted by the extremely thick glaze.

This copy of a 13thC Yingqing dish is too deep and lacks the subtle contours of the original; and the forger has been over-enthusiastic in his moulding.
* The rim has been dressed in iron-red to simulate the oxidization.

Marks

The mark is the last thing to look at on Chinese porcelain. The vast majority of pieces are inscribed with an earlier mark, and it is only possible to tell whether the mark is contemporaneous with the piece after many years of experience with calligraphy.

GERMAN PORCELAIN

Most German fakes and forgeries were intended to be mistaken for 18thC Meissen. Throughout the 19thC, many German factories continued to make copies of 18thC Meissen products and to inscribe them with similar or identical marks. They were so popular that even Meissen made copies, which were at least better than the others.

During the 18thC, Meissen wares were faked by several minor factories in Thuringia, where they were inscribed with spurious crossed-swords marks. They were also imitated in England. For example, the Derby factory used Chinese Meissen wares as models; and in c.1755 the Chelsea factory copied a whole consignment of Meissen wares and figures. During the 19thC, a considerable number of factories produced excellent imitations of Meissen. One of the best was Carl Thieme's factory in Potschappel, and another was the Dresden factory of Helena Wolfshon, who copied Meissen wares of the 1740s and even added the Augustus Rex mark, until Meissen obtained an injunction against her, forcing her to change the mark to a crown above the word Dresden.

Both this *bonbonnière* and the cat's head cane handle were made by Edmé Samson of Paris, who started his career in 1845 as a decorator of white porcelains from other factories. In the 1850s, he set up a hard-paste factory in Montreuil and began to make his own porcelain copies.
* The cat and the pug dog are very well decorated, but they are slightly over-elaborate, and the use of colour is on the whole insensitive compared with the originals'.
* A close look at the unglazed areas on both pieces reveals the smooth, greyish paste of the Samson factory, which is not at all like the dirty and gouged surface on most genuine Meissen footrims.

Neither the pug nor the cat was intended to deceive. They are both fully marked with Samson's crossed batons, and are inscribed "*Modèle Samson*".

Probably the most successful, and the most collectable, Samson copies are his Meissen figures after Eberlein or Kändler. This version of Eberlein's Tyrolean dancers is accurately modelled and coloured, but there are differences in the pigments: the man's breeches are the wrong shade of blue, and the girl's bodice is the wrong turquoise.
* Early Meissen figures are meticulously decorated. The hair in particular is very finely detailed. The thick brushstrokes which Samson's painters have

used would only be found on 19thC Meissen.

* Samson's surface is relatively smooth compared with Meissen's, and his glaze is much glassier. However, the most obvious differences are in the base: Samson's painters have not quite captured the yellowish green foliage which typifies early Meissen. Also, Meissen bases are often quite sharp-edged, whereas Samson's tend to be subtly rounded.

* Samson copies often have pieces of very fine kiln grit on the perimeter of the base.

Samson's version of a Meissen saucer decorated by J.G. Herold (*above top*) is in many ways an excellent copy and may have been made as a replacement. The colours are almost right, but the gilding on the rim is weak, the porcelain ground is white rather than greyish and the whole decoration has none of the boisterous baroque mood of the original (*above bottom*).

* The original is also thinly potted, whereas the copy is quite thick.

This Samson model of the advocate from the *Commedia dell'Arte* is quite convincing, but it lacks the original's sharpness.

There is a small, unglazed patch on the rear of the advocate's base where the Samson mark has been ground away. This is also the place which would have been marked with crossed swords if the figure had been genuine.

Unlike the Samson copy, this version of a Herold plate is a brilliant forgery. Probably made in the 1950s, the decoration is based on a motif from Herold's book of drawings and is painted with great panache on a stripped Meissen plate, made between 1740 and 50 and originally decorated with sprigs of flowers. The only clues to the misrepresentation lie in the scratches and the "ghosts" of a few leaves, which show when the plate is held to the light.

FRENCH PORCELAIN

Sèvres

Ever since the French royal factory moved from Vincennes to Sèvres, in 1756, its porcelain has been copied and faked by almost every European factory.

When the factory was founded, its declared purpose was to make porcelain in the manner of Meissen, but 15 years later the roles were reversed and even Meissen was copying Sèvres. Very few of the early copies were made with any intention to deceive, and almost all of them are easy to detect. But after the Revolution tons of white wares were sold off to outside decorators in England as well as France; and on many of these the enamelling is so effective that it has even deceived experts. Some later-decorated pieces are very fine and currently undervalued.

In England the fashion for Sèvres never died out. In 1813, the new Nantgarw factory produced moulded wares in Sèvres' old Rococo style. Thomas Martin Randall, who was decorating white wares at about the same time, specialized in imitations of Sèvres. By the middle of the century Coalport and Minton were making accurate copies of the large decorative pieces which Sèvres had made a hundred years earlier, and Minton was actually using a Sèvres mark.

Those copies, which, like the ones by Randall, were painted on original Sèvres wares, can be difficult to detect, but other copies and fakes present few difficulties:-
* Most of them are made of hard-paste porcelain and not soft-paste like Sèvres.
* Although most Sèvres fakes are marked with interlaced "Ls", very few have date letters like the originals.
* Sèvres had very stringent quality controls. If the piece has the slightest flaw, the best it can be is a reject which has been decorated later.
* The gilding on Sèvres copies and fakes is often brassy and flat, and it is very seldom up to the standard of the original, which was the best.

Other factories

At the end of the 19thC and the beginning of the 20thC, a number of Paris hard-paste factories produced copies of Chantilly, St Cloud and other early soft-paste wares. By far the best were made by Emil Samson, the son of Edmé, but, like all the others, he was betrayed by his paste.

This large "Sèvres" vase was made in Paris, c.1870. The dark blue ground and the quality of the painting are very convincing, but the quality of the gilding is not up to Sèvres' supreme standard.

The St Cloud factory produced some of the loveliest porcelain in France with a warm creamy glaze. As he could not use a soft-paste, Emil Samson attempted to reproduce it here in a *faïence fine*. However, *faïence* is very difficult to pot neatly. The granular body, inaccurate potting and clumsily applied flowers have all given this pot away.
* This piece is marked with the St Cloud monogran, STC, but this is hardly deceptive as it also has Emil Samson's interlaced Ss incised crudely on the base.

Chantilly is perhaps the most easily recognized of all the French porcelains. For about the first 25 years of its manufacture, it was covered in a tin glaze, which gave a very sharp outline to the Kakiemon-style pieces which made up the bulk of the factory's production. This Samson copy has been painted with a similar precision to the original, but the colours in the Samson palette are too vibrant, and of course the greyish white hard-paste body immediately identifies it.
* The piece is marked with the Chantilly hunting horn and also the entwined Ss, of the Samson factory, both of which have been painted in red enamel.

In some ways this "Chantilly" flower pot is more convincing than the bowl. It is made of an extremely fine porcellaneous material and it is covered in a thin tin glaze. The decoration is also appropriately precise. However, the decorator has painted the swags very much in the style of early Art Deco, underlining the fact that most people find it difficult to work in the style of a period other than the one that they live in.
* Although full names and signatures were never used at Chantilly, the flat base is inscribed unintelligibly with the name of a manufacturer.

In the second half of the 19thC, many of the Paris factories produced large Neo-classical "Sèvres" vases, usually with *bleu celeste* grounds. Some were decorated with scenes commemorating the career of Napoleon, but many more were decorated after Watteau and Boucher.

This is a genuine Sèvres piece with a ground down footrim, but the areas of fine speckling indicate that it has been refired and therefore that the decoration has been added later.

171

Chelsea

Chelsea porcelain of the red anchor period (see pp.114-115) is probably the finest of the factory's production in terms of taste and decorative appeal. During this period fruit, vegetables and animals were a favourite theme for tureens – a life-size rabbit tureen is mentioned in the Chelsea sale catalogue of 1758 – and at the end of the 19thC these shapes became equally popular with copyists in both England and France, particularly at the Samson factory in Paris.

The rabbit tureen *above*, made by Samson c.1870-1900, is in hard-paste porcelain – which immediately identifies it as a copy: the original would have been in soft-paste. It is marked with Samson's interlaced "S"'s in blue enamel.

anchor, which suggests that in this case Samson was attempting to deceive. Samson animals are particularly collectable.

This is a copy of a Chelsea piece of around 1755, which was itself based on a Meissen piece. It was made in a house in Union Street, Torquay, by Reginald Newland between 1950 and 1971. Newland made a lot of pieces like this, and when they first appeared on the market they fooled several experts because of their slightly primitive look and the number of firing flaws, or fissures, in the body of their porcelain. Their pale washed-out colours and their heavy potting also made them very similar to early products not only from Chelsea but also from Derby and Bow. Newland was exposed when one of his Derby squirrels was compared with a known original.

This is a Samson copy of a 1755 billing dove tureen, made c.1900. Like most of his "Chelsea" copies, it is of high quality and is only let down by the insensitive application of flowers and as always, the Samson hard-paste, which is nothing like Chelsea's creamy soft-paste. It is marked on the base with a spurious brown

Worcester

The Japanese patterns of Worcester have always been popular with copyists, especially in Paris. There are large numbers of blue-scale wares with spurious seal marks in circulation. However, these are simple to detect, as Worcester's soaprock porcelain has a distinctive grainy and greyish look, while the copies are almost always slick and glassy.

* There are fewer copies and fakes of the wares decorated by James Giles.
* During the 19thC Worcester made many hard-paste copies of its own early soft-paste wares.
* Even today a number of copyists are producing hard-paste versions of Worcester blue and white wares.

This copy of a bell-shaped Chamberlain's Worcester mug was made at the Samson factory in Paris around the end of the 19thC. The *famille verte* palette and even the gilding are quite close to the Worcester original, but as always the porcelain is Samson's tell-tale hard-paste.

This supposedly Worcester lettuce-leaf sauceboat from the late 1750s is in fact French and was made around 1900 or later. It is not convincing:-
* It is made of glassy hard-paste.
* The strange limey green and electric puce are not Worcester factory colours.
* The neat, regimented distribution of insects is not in the style of an 18thC painter.
* The moulded decoration is not sharp enough to be either Worcester or 18thC.

The Booth's factory in Tunstall made a large number of reproductions of Worcester blue scale wares. The were inscribed with the factory's mark, but even without this there are several reasons why they are unlikely to be mistaken for the originals:-
* They are made of fine earthenware, which is slightly brown.
* The designs are transfer printed, which makes them rather dull and lifeless.
* The proportions are all wrong. In this case the upper half of the sparrow-beak jug is far too wide.

Bow

There are relatively few copies of Bow porcelain. Samson and the other French copyists tended to ignore the factory, although it did not escape the attentions of Reginald Newland and one or two other unknown artists. A fake Bow figure of a Thames waterman appeared on the market comparatively recently.

This is an extremely accurate copy of a Bow blue and white dish of 1750, which was in turn copied from Chinese export ware. Although it is made of hard-paste, the decoration is excellent, if only because the Bow version was also stiffly painted. Like the original, it has the marks where it was fired on three small spurs on the upper rim.

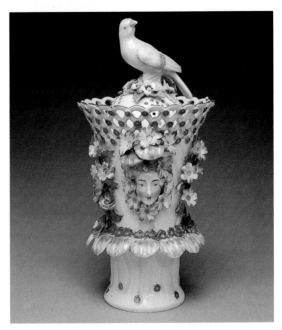

Derby

Only a few Derby pieces were copied, but they were copied quite often and by many different copyists. There are a number of English country houses which contain one of Samson's versions of the frill vase, like the one *above*.

For several reasons, this vase is not as convincing as some of Samson's other copies:-
* The colours are right but the tones are wrong. For example, the puce is too harsh and the blue is too grey.
* The Samson material is too glassy.
* The applied florets are very mean-looking and they have been applied much too evenly and mechanically.
* The human mask on the side is too even-featured to have been made in the 18thC.
* The base is marked incorrectly with the gold anchor of Chelsea – a common mistake – and it does not have the three patch marks which all Derby pieces have as a result of the factory's firing methods.

Longton Hall

The only person known to have copied Longton Hall porcelain was Reginald Newland of Torquay. Some of his pieces are so convincing that they have appeared in books on the factory. However, there are hard-paste versions of Longton Hall wares made at Plymouth, which acquired the moulds in 1760.

These copies of middle-period Longton Hall melon tureens, made by Newland in the early 1950s, are among the pieces that have fooled even leading experts, but the very pale, washed-out puce and green are totally unconvincing. However, because of their quality, Newland pieces are worth looking at in their own right.

Plymouth

Plymouth wares present a special problem because Cookworthy used only hard-paste porcelain, like the copyists and forgers. Large numbers of forgeries of Plymouth wares were made in Paris at the turn of the century, which is at first surprising, since Plymouth was a small factory which lasted for only two years. However, this of course makes its wares rare and therefore valuable to collectors – and fakes of valuable wares are the only ones which are worth the forgers' effort. However, the forgers were usually let down by their palette. The Plymouth palette is eccentric and has a mushroom brown which seems to be unique to the factory.

Shell salts were produced in large numbers by the Plymouth factory, but because of their mass of clay and their almost architectural structure, they tended to split in the firing and most of them are slightly distorted. However, this fake is neat and well potted, and it has hardly a flaw. It therefore fails because it is *too* well made; and it also fails because the palette is too washed-out.

On even the most cursory examination, this "Plymouth" tankard would be betrayed by its smooth surface and even potting – that is, if the rather weak flower painting and the inappropriate palette had not already done so.

Lowestoft

Lowestoft commemorative pieces, both blue and white and *famille rose* were faked in some numbers early in this century.

These are only two out of a very large number of "Lowestoft" mugs which are all inscribed "Abraham Moore, August 29, 1765". The fact that they all bear the same commemoration is in itself enough to reveal them as fakes, but they have other unconvincing features:
* The underglaze blue is very runny and the glaze is a bit crackled, neither of which was characteristic of Lowestoft.
* Although the shape is more or less correct, the mugs are quite heavily potted and are made of a greyish paste, whereas the true Lowestoft mugs are thinly potted in a white paste and have brownish discolorations.
* There is a growing interest in "documentary" porcelain as examples of the forger's art.

Copies of Welsh porcelain

The Samson factory made copies of both Nantgarw and Swansea wares and printed or impressed them with the appropriate factory marks. The Samson hard-paste is quite close to the Swansea paste, but it is not as creamy.

This slightly over-bright forgery of a Swansea plate was probably made in Paris c.1860.

MARKS

Most European porcelain manufacturers marked their wares with an identifying symbol; a shield, a crown or some other device. Most marks are straightforward, the crossed swords of Meissen and the interlaced L's of Sèvres (formerly Vincennes) are the most well-known marks, and the most copied. It would be impossible to show all the relevant marks in a book of this size, although many of the most important ones are shown or described throughout the book. Specialist books are available that deal solely with marks. However, many minor concerns aped the more fashionable factories. In addition, many early marks were applied by hand, so no two are exactly alike. Thus the mark has to be treated with extreme caution and an attribution made only after the other criteria have been met. The following is a list of letters and symbols used by major European and American manufacturers. The letter may be the only mark or it might be employed in tandem with some other device. Oriental reign marks are shown on p.19.

Single letters

A Ansback, Amstel, Bow, Paris, St Cloud, Copenhagen, Fulda.
B Bow, Frankenthal, Worcester, Bristol.
C Caughley, Orleans. Beware of the crescent mark of Worcester which resembles the C of Caughley.
D Davenport, Derby, Limoges.
F Fürstenberg, Frankenthal, Fulda, Bow, Longton Hall, Copenhagen.
G Bow, Buen Retiro (offshoot of Capodimonte), Gotha, Gera
H Limoges, Paris, Strasbourg.
I Ilmenau, Bow, St Cloud.
J Longton Hall
L Paris, Ludwigsburg, Longton Hall (interlaced or addorsed Ls similar to crossed swords), Limback (similar to previous).
M Minton
N New Hall, Limback, Derby, Naples, Volkstedt.
O Orleans
P Pinxton, Liverpool, Chantilly, Nymphenburg, Bonnin & Morris
R Rauenstein, Gotha, Bow, Selb, Thuringia, Limoges.
S Caughley, Nymphenburg, St Cloud, Thuringia (various)
T Bow, Bristol
V Venice
W Worcester, Würzburg, Wallendorf, Berlin, Vienna
X Fulda, Bristol

Letters in combination

AL Alcora (Spain); AM Aich (Bavaria); AR Meissen, Wolfshon (Dresden); AS Eisenback
BD and BL Orleans; BFB Worcester; BG Copenhagen
CD Coalbrookdale;
CD/CFH Limoges; CG Copeland; CT Frankenthal; CV Closter-Veilsdorf;
FBB Worcester; FR Pirkenhammer
GDM/GR Limoges; GP Gotha
JH Worcester; Strasbourg (here the J is written in the old style as 'i'); JP Jacob Petit (Paris); JPL Limoges
KHC Meissen; KPM Berlin: Waldenburg
LB Limbach
MB Marieberg; M:oL Oude Loosdrecht
PH Strasbourg (and Frankenthal) and Thuringia;
PN Pinxton
RF République Française, Sèvres
SCT St Cloud; SP and SX Sceaux
VR(F) Frankenthal
Z Zürich

Common symbols

Anchor: Chelsea, Bow, Cozzi (Venice), Samson, Davenport, Derby, and various minor 19thC Thuringian factories.
Antlers: Ludwigsburg
Crescent: Worcester, copied by Caughley, Lowestoft, Liverpool
Crossed swords: Meissen, Tournai (with crosses in the angles), Weesp (with dots in the angles)
Crown: Derby, Vincennes and Sèvres, Buen Retiro, Chelsea, Frankenthal, Ludwigsburg, Höchst, Tournai and others.
Fleur-de-lis: Capodimonte
Hunting horn: Chantilly
Shield: Nymphenburg (with diamond-shaped network), Vienna
Star: Doccia
Sun with face: St Cloud
Triangle: Chelsea
Wheel: Höchst

GLOSSARY

Acid gilding A decorative process whereby patterns are etched into porcelain with hydrofluoric acid, then **gilded** and burnished.

American Belleek A late-19thC American version of the thinly-potted wares originally made at the Irish Belleek factory.

Enamel Overglaze colours made from metallic oxides.

Applied moulding Relief decoration made separately from the body and applied later.

Arcanist One who possesses a porcelain formula – from *arcanum*, the Latin for mystery.

Arita An area of western Kyushu, where most early Japanese porcelain was made from c.1610, including **Imari, Blue and white, Kakiemon,** and **Nabeshima.**

Armorial wares Wares decorated with coats-of-arms or crests, either **transfer-printed** or painted. Usually, refers to Chinese porcelain bearing European coats-of-arms, produced from 16thC.

Artificial porcelain Another term for **soft-paste** porcelain.

A tulipano A pattern devised at the Doccia factory, depicting sprays of peonies in a formal Oriental style.

Baluster vase A vase shape resembling the curved support of a balustrade.

Baroque A vigorous decorative style that grew out of the Renaissance, characterized by lively figures and symmetrical ornament. Meissen's porcelain of the early 18thC is the most notable.

Basketweave A relief pattern resembling woven willow twigs (oziers) used on borders by most European factories in the 1730s.

Bat-printing A type of **transfer-printing** used by early 19thC Staffordshire firms. The design was transferred from an engraved plate to a glazed surface via slabs of glue or gelatin (bats).

Birnkrug A pear-shaped jug or mug. Originally produced in Dutch or German earthenware and stoneware (in the 17thC), it was later adopted by the early porcelain factories.

Biscuit Unglazed porcelain or **earthenware** fired once only. The term also refers to white porcelain (especially figures) left unglazed and undecorated.

Blackware A type of ancient Chinese ceramics similar to **greenware**, but with more iron in the formula. See also Chinese **whiteware**.

Blanc de Chine A translucent white Chinese porcelain, unpainted and with a thick glaze. It was made at kilns in Dehua in the Fukien province, from the Ming dynasty, and often copied in Europe.

Bleu celeste A sky-blue **ground** colour developed by Jean Hellot at Vincennes in 1752.

Bleu-du-roi Also *bleu nouveau.* A rich blue **enamel** used as a **ground** colour at Sevres.

Bleu lapis Also *gros bleu.* An intense cobalt blue **ground** of almost purplish tone, introduced at Vincennes in 1749.

Blue and white The term for any white Oriental or Western porcelain decorated with cobalt blue enamel.

Blue scale A decorative pattern of blue overlapping scales.

Bocage Densely-encrusted flowering tree-stumps supporting a group or used as a backdrop.

Body The material from which **pottery** or **porcelain** is made (although the term **paste** is more often used for porcelain). Also refers to the main part of a piece.

Bonbonnière A small box or covered bowl for sweetmeats, often in novelty form.

Bone ash Burnt, crushed animal bone that is added to **soft-paste** mixture to fuse the ingredients. The process was introduced c.1750 at Bow and other English factories.

Bone china A porcelain recipe consisting of **petuntse, kaolin** and dried bone, supposedly invented by Josiah Spode II in c.1794. It became the mainstay of the English porcelain industry from c.1820.

Botanical wares Wares decorated with painted flowers, generally copied from prints or engravings.

Bracket lobes Bracket-shaped moulding used on dish rims.

Brocade Decorative patterns derived from textiles, employing repeated geometric motifs, abstract designs, or reserves enclosing animal, figural or floral subjects set against a contrasting (usually floral) **ground.**

Cachepot An ornamental container for ordinary flower pots. A smaller form of *jardinière*.

Caillouté Literally, "pebbled". An irregular pattern of amorphous oblongs picked out in gilding on a solid ground.

Camaieu Painted decoration in different tones of one colour. See also *grisaille.*

Campana vase An inverted, bell-shaped vase (sometimes with a handle on each shoulder).

Canton porcelain The term for wares produced and enamelled in Canton province for export to the West. Usually heavily decorated with reserves of figures, flowers, birds and butterflies on a complex ground of green, pink and gold scrolling foliage.

Cartouche A decorative motif in the form of a scroll of paper with rolled ends, bearing a picture, motif or monogram. Also used to describe a frame, usually oval, decorated with scrollwork. See also *vignette.*

Cash pattern A Chinese repeat pattern based on the design of Chinese coins with a square central hole. Also known as coin pattern.

Celadon A semi-opaque glaze, usually grey-green, applied to Chinese **stoneware** before firing.

Chiaroscuro The term for decorative use of contrasting shade and light.

China A general term for **porcelain**, derived from the "China wares" imported into Europe from 16thC. In 19thC England it came to mean almost any porcelain-like ceramic.

China clay Another term for **kaolin**, a white clay mixed with **petuntse** to form **true porcelain.**

Chinese export porcelain Chinese **hard-paste** porcelain made from the 16thC to suit European tastes. Also known as "China trade porcelain".

Chinese Imari Chinese copies or pastiches of Japanese Imari wares, made largely for export from c.1700. The decoration involves Japanese **brocade** designs and the typical Imari palette of dark **underglaze blue**, iron-red and gilt, with no **spur marks.**

Chinoiserie The European fashion for Chinese decoration and motifs, influential in all areas of the decorative arts in the 18thC.

Cisele gilding Thickly-applied gilding with patterns tooled in to increase the decorative effect.

Clobbering The Dutch term for the practice of over-printing blue and white Oriental porcelain in colour enamels with designs rarely compatible with the original theme.

Cloud pattern An incised or painted scrolled design, often of square form, on Chinese porcelain.

Cobalt blue A pigment used in blue and white decoration.

Colloidal gold A form of gold solution, used in **gilding.**

Comb pattern A pattern, often painted in **underglaze** blue, that looks as if it has been made with a toothed comb. Found mainly on **Nabeshima** porcelain.

Commedia dell'Arte A traditional Italian comedy, with characters extemporising on a general theme. The characters were modelled in porcelain by Meissen, Nymphenburg and other factories.

Crackle A network of fine cracks introduced as decoration into the glazing of some Chinese Song dynasty porcelain and later copies.

Craze Tiny, undesirable surface cracks caused by shrinking in the glaze, or other technical defects.

Delftware Tin-glazed earthenware made in England (called **faïence** in Germany, France and Scandinavia). When capitalized as Delftware, it refers to the same type of wares made in the Netherlands.

Deutsche Blumen Painted flowers, single or in bunches, used as decoration in the mid-18thC. The style is derived from botanical wood-block prints.

Diaper A pattern of repeated diamonds or other geometrical shapes seen on Chinese porcelain.

Ding Yao A type of **porcelain** made in China during the 10thC Sung dynasty, with a creamy-white body and an orange translucence.

Documentary piece Wares that bear evidence indicating the origin of the piece, such as the signature of the decorator or modeller, or an **armorial** mark.

Doucai A form of decoration using **overglaze enamels** (specifically red, yellow, brown, green and black) within an **underglaze blue** outline. First used in 15thC China.

Dry edge An unglazed area around the base of some early Derby figures.

Earthenware Non-vitreous pottery that is not **stoneware**. See also **tin-glazed earthenware.**

Faïence see Delftware

Famille jaune A type of *famille verte,* featuring a yellow ground.

Famille noire A variant of the 17th and 18thC Chinese *famille verte* palette, with **reserves** set against a black background.

Famille rose A palette dominated by opaque rose pink enamel.

Famille verte A type of 17th and 18thC Chinese decoration largely based on brilliant green enamels. Much copied on European earthenware and some porcelain.

Fan-shaped or **scroll-shaped reserves** Reserves in the form of

Oriental scrolls, often fan-shaped, bearing writing or painting.

Feldspar A rock-forming mineral (also known as Chinese **petuntse**) used to make **hard-paste porcelain**. Feldspar china, a variant of **bone china**, was made from c.1820. Feldspathic glazes applied to hard-paste porcelain become glassy (vitreous) at high temperatures.

Fêtes galantes The term for open-air scenes of aristocratic amusement that were a favourite theme of French Rococo painters.

Fire cracks The term for the splitting in the body that can appear after firing. Usually regarded as acceptable damage.

Firing The process of baking ceramics in a kiln. Temperatures range from 800°C (1472°F) for **earthenware** to 1450°C (2642°F) for some **hard-paste porcelain** and stoneware.

Flambe **glaze** A Chinese glaze made from reduced copper, dating from the Song dynasty. It is usually deep crimson, flecked with blue or purple, and often faintly crackled. It was also used on 18thC Chinese porcelain and copied in Europe.

Flatware Flat or shallow wares such as plates, dishes and saucers. See also **hollow ware.**

Fluting A pattern of concave grooves repeated in vertical, parallel lines. The inverse of **gadroon**.

Footrim A projecting circular base on the underside of a plate or vessel. *See also* **undercut.**

Frit The powdered glass added to fine white clay to make a type of soft-paste porcelain.

Gadroon Decorative edging consisting of a series of convex, vertical or spiralling curves.

Galanterien Small portable wares such as snuffboxes, necessaires, patch boxes and scent bottles, sometimes in the form of figures, animals or fruit.

Galletto A decorative pattern of red and gold Chinese cockerels, devised at the Doccia factory.

Garniture de cheminée A set of three or more vases of contrasting forms, intended for mantelpiece display.

Gilding The application of gold leaf or gold mixed with honey or mercury. See also **acid-gilding, cisele-gilding** and **gloss-gilding.**

Glaze A glassy coating painted, dusted or sprayed onto the surface of porcelain and **stoneware** which becomes smooth and shiny after firing, making the body non-porous.

Gloss-gilding The **gilding** of porcelain using gold in solution.

"Green" The term for unfired wares. Not to be confused with Chinese **greenware**.

Greenware High-fired Chinese ceramics with a green glaze, dating from the Shang dynasty. Also called **celadon** wares.

Grisaille Painted decoration using a mainly black and grey palette and resembling a print.

Ground The base or background colour on a body, to which decoration and gilding are applied.

Guanyao Official **stoneware** of the Song dynasty.

Guilloche A Neo-classical pattern of twisting bands, spirals, double spirals or linked chains.

Hans Sloane wares A type of wares produced at the Chelsea factory from 1752-57.

Hard-paste porcelain The technical term for porcelain made according to the Chinese formula combining **kaolin** and **petuntse**.

Hausmaler The German term for an independent painter or workshop specializing in the decoration of **blanks**, especially from Meissen.

"Heaping and piling" Accidental concentrations of cobalt blue in 14thC and 15thC Chinese **blue and white** porcelain.

Hirado A type of Japanese **blue and white** porcelain made in the Arita district from the mid-18thC. The wares have a distinctive, milky-white body, a velvet-like glaze and superlative pictorial decoration.

"Hob in the well" A pattern used on Japanese **Kakiemon** ware and much copied in Europe, based on a Song dynasty legend.

Hongs Warehouses erected in China by European traders and used for storing goods for export.

Hookah or **narghileh** A type of Middle-Eastern smoking pipe. See also **Kendi.**

Huashi Literally, "slippery stone". The Chinese term for a type of **soft-paste** porcelain most often used for small, finely decorated pieces.

Imari A type of Japanese porcelain made in the Arita district in the 17th and 18thC and exported from the port of Imari. Features dense **brocade** patterns and a **palette** of **underglaze** blue, iron-red and **gilding**.

Imperial wares Wares produced in China at least as early as the Northern Song dynasty (980-1127) intended for the home market.

Impressed Indented, as opposed to **incised**. Used of marks and hallmarks.

Incised Scratched into the surface. Used of marks and decoration.

Indianische Blumen The German term for floral decoration on Meissen porcelain derived from Kakiemon styles. Generally 1720-1740.

"In the white" or **blanks** Undecorated porcelain wares.

Japonaise or **Japanesque** The term for European designs c.1862-1900, inspired by Japanese decoration.

Jardiniere See *cachepot.*

Jasper ware A hard, fine-grained red **stoneware** introduced at Meissen by Böttger in the early 18thC.

Jewelled decoration A decorative method whereby drops of translucent **enamel** are applied over gold or silver foil, in imitation of precious gems.

Kaga The district of Japan where **Kutani** wares were made.

Kakiemon A much-copied decorative style introduced by the Kakiemon family in the Arita district of Japan during the 17thC. Typically, sparse and asymmetrical decoration is executed in a vivid palette on a dead-white *nigoshide* ground.

Kaolin A fine white china clay used to make **true porcelain.**

Kendi The Persian word for a globular-bodied porcelain drinking vessel with a short spout, made in 15th and 16thC China for export to the Middle East. See also **Hookah.**

Kickback terminal A handle that terminates in a flourish away from the body of the piece.

Kinrande The term for a Japanese pattern of gilt on a red ground that originated in mid-16thC China and was much copied in Japan.

Knop Literally, the bud of a flower. Refers to the decorative knobs on teapot and vase covers.

Ko-Kutani see **Kutani**

Ko-sumetsuke The Japanese term for "old blue and white" porcelain imported from China during the late Ming dynasty. See also **Blue and white** and **Hirado**

Kraak-porselein The Dutch term for late Ming Chinese blue and white porcelain that was mass-produced for export to Europe. Also, the segmented patterns which typically decorated the borders of the flatwares.

Kutani A type of Japanese porcelain. Old, or *"ko" kutani* was allegedly made at Kutani in Kaga province in the early 17thC,

although most, if not all, was made in **Arita** in a so-called Kutani style. The style was revived in the 19thC as *ao-Kutani* (green kutani).

Kylin A dragon-headed beast with the body and limbs of a deer and a lion's tail. In Chinese mythology it is a symbol of goodness. Also known as a *ch'ilin* or *qilin.*

Kyoto A centre of porcelain making in 19thC Japan.

Lambrequins The French term for Baroque border patterns of lacework, scrolls and scalloped drapery.

Lang yao See *Sang-de-boeuf.*

Laub und bandelwerk Literally "leaf and strapwork". The German term for Baroque **cartouches** that surround a pictorial **reserve.**

Leys jars A type of large rounded wine-jar with shoulder handles.

Lingzhi A fungus symbolizing longevity; a common 16thC Chinese decorative motif.

Li shui A type of Sung dynasty **celadon** wares.

Lithophane A kind of thin, low relief pictorial plaque that reveals a **chiaroscuro** effect when held up to the light. Also called "Berlin transparencies".

Mandarin pattern A mainly red and purple decoration of figures within complicated **diaper** borders, often found on Chinese export **porcelain** of the mid-18th to the early 19thC.

Manganese A mineral used to make purple brown pigments.

Masso bastardo Italian term for a poor-quality **hard-paste** made at the Doccia factory in the 18thC. Its rough, sticky, grey surface often shows **fire cracks.**

Mazarin blue The English version of Sevres *gros bleu,* introduced in the late 1750s.

Meiping A high-shouldered, short and narrow-necked Chinese **baluster** vase, designed to hold a single flower spray.

Millefleurs The French term for a type of dense floral decoration.

Mon A Japanese insignia.

Monochrome Decoration executed in one colour.

Moons Air bubbles in the **body** (or **paste**) which expand during the firing of incorrectly formulated porcelain (generally **soft-paste**), leaving translucent spots.

Mount A decorative ormolu or gilt-bronze attachment to porcelain.

Muffle The chamber inside a kiln that prevents wares from being damaged by flames during firing.

Nabeshima wares Arita wares made from the mid-17thC at

Okawachi. Palettes consist of black and white, coloured enamels or celadon.

Neo-classical A decorative style, based on a revival of Etruscan, Greek, Egyptian or Roman ornament.

Nigoshide The dead-white body and colourless glaze used for the best quality **Kakiemon** porcelain.

Oeil de perdrix Literally, "eye of a partridge"; a pattern of dotted circles in enamel or gilding, used at Sèvres and copied by Meissen.

Ollientopfe A type of ceramic broth bowl.

Ormolu A gilded, brass-like alloy of copper, zinc and tin, used for mounts on fine furniture and other decoration.

Overglaze The term for any porcelain decoration painted in enamels or **transfer-printed** on top of a fired glaze.

Ozier See **basketweave**

Palette The range of colours used in the decoration of a piece, or favoured by a factory or decorator. The term also includes gilding.

Parian A semi-matt biscuit porcelain made from **feldspar** and **china clay**. Originally called "statuary porcelain", it became known as "Parian" because of its similarity to the white marble from the Greek island of Paros.

Paste The mixture of ingredients from which **porcelain** is made.

Pâte-sur-pâte A kind of porcelain decoration involving low-relief designs carved in **slip** and applied in layers to a contrasting body.

Peach bloom A vari-coloured glaze derived from copper. Ranging in hue from red to green, it was seen first on Chinese **Kangxi** wares.

Petit feu **enamels** Colours applied at low temperatures.

Petuntse Or "china stone". A fusible, feldspathic bonding mineral used to make **hard-paste porcelain**.

Pierced decoration A method of decoration whereby a pattern is cut out of the body with a knife prior to firing.

Plasticity A term to describe the pliability of a china clay.

Pointilliste A style of painting involving the application of tiny dots of colour.

Polychrome Decoration executed in more than two colours. See **Wucai** and **doucai**

Porcelain A translucent white ceramic body fired at a high temperature. The formula can be either **hard-paste** or **soft-paste**.

Potiche The French word for a small porcelain vase or lidded jar.

Powder-blue A mottled blue **ground** achieved by blowing dry pigment onto a piece through gauze.

Porcellaneous A piece with some of the ingredients or features of **porcelain** but which is not necessarily translucent.

Press-moulding The moulding of figures or applied ornament achieved by pressing clay into an absorbent mould.

Puce A purple red colour formed from **manganese** oxide.

Punch'ong A type of greyish coarse **celadon** stoneware, usually coated in **slip**, made in south Korea during the 15th and 16thC.

Pu-Tai Ho-shang Also known as Budai Heshang or the "laughing Buddha". The figure of a grinning pot-bellied monk sitting cross-legged on a cushion. Appears on Chinese porcelain or as a statuette.

Putti Decorative motifs of small, naked, male baby-like figures.

Quatrefoil A shape or design incorporating four foils, or lobes (hence also quatrelobe).

Reeding A milled edge, or parallel pattern in the form of reeds.

Reliefzierat German term for the shallow moulded relief decoration used notably on Berlin wares.

Reign marks Marks applied to some Chinese porcelain to denote the emperor during whose reign the piece was made.

Reserve A self-contained blank area within a pattern, reserved for other decoration.

Robin's egg glaze A pale blue, speckled glaze developed in China during the early-mid 18thC.

Rococo A decorative European style that evolved in the early 18thC from the Baroque. Typically featured asymmetric ornament and flamboyant scrollwork.

Rose medallion See **Canton porcelain**

Rose Pompadour A dealer's term for the rich, deep pink glaze used by Sèvres as a ground colour from c.1757-64. Named after Louise XV's famous mistress, Madame du Pompadour.

Saltglaze A thin, glassy, non-porous glaze applied to some **stoneware** by throwing salt into the kiln at the height of firing.

Sang-de-boeuf Literally "ox-blood". A bright red glaze, toning to darker areas, first used during the Qing dynasty in China.

Satsuma A major Japanese port famed for its crackle-glazed ceramics.

Schwarzlot A type of linear

painting in black developed in Germany.

Scroll feet A type of base that incorporates a scroll motif, either in shape or in decoration.

Seladon fond Meissen's sea-green **ground** used to decorate wares in the 1730s. See also celadon wares.

Sgraffito The term for patterns incised into the **slip** surface of a piece exposing the contrasting body underneath.

Shoki-Imari "Early **Imari**" wares.

Shonzui A type of 17thC Ming export porcelain made for the Japanese market and decorated with **brocade** patterns and **diapers**.

Shu fu Opaque white **porcelain** with a matte, blue-tinged glaze made at Jingdezhen in Yuan dynasty China and incised with the characters "shu fu", meaning "Privy Council".

Sleeve vase A long, thin cylindrical vase.

slip A mixture of clay and water used for decorating ceramic bodies and for **slip-casting** and **sprigging**.

Soapstone or **soaprock** A type of steatite used instead of **kaolin** in **soft-paste** porcelain from 1750.

Soft-paste or **artificial porcelain** A **porcelain** formula made from a mixture of **(frit)**, **soapstone** and **bone ash**. See also **hard-paste**.

Sprigged wares The term for wares decorated with small, low-relief moulding applied with **slip**.

Stilt marks or **spur marks** Small defects on the base or **footrim** of a piece made by the supporting stilts (or cockspurs) used during firing.

Stampino An Italian term for blue and white stencil decorations.

Stoneware Ceramic wares of clay and sand or flint, fired at a higher temperature to earthenware (c.1350°C), making it durable and non-porous. Pieces are often **salt-glazed** or left unglazed and, if thinly potted, are as translucent as porcelain.

"Sumptuary Laws" Laws introduced by Louis XV c.1750, forbidding the use of gilding in porcelain decoration and discouraging competition with the Royal factory at Sèvres.

Swag A decorative motif of looped flowers or foliage.

Temmoku The Japanese term for a molasses-coloured glaze used in the Chinese province of Henan from the Song period; made from iron oxide.

Théière calabre The term for a certain shape of Sèvres teapot.

Thumbpieces The angled

attachment to the upper part of a cup handle.

Thrown wares Hollow wares shaped on a pottery wheel.

Tin-glaze An opaque, glassy, white glaze made from tin oxide; commonly used on earthenware bodies such as **delftware**, *faïence* and maiolica.

Transfer-printing A decorative technique whereby a design can be mass-produced by transferring it from an inked engraving onto paper and then to a ceramic body.

Transitional porcelain The term for porcelain produced in Jingdezhen, China, between the end of the Ming dynasty and the start of the Qing (1620-50).

Trompe d'oeil Pictorial decoration intended to deceive the eye.

Tureen A deep soup dish with cover.

Undercut foot The term for an inward-sloping base to a piece.

Underglaze A coloured sheath or pattern applied to **biscuit** porcelain before glazing and firing.

Veilleuse A food warmer comprising a vessel over a source of heat.

Vert pomme A mid-green enamel **ground** introduced at Sèvres c.1756.

Vignette An area of design or a picture that merges into the surrounding area.

Violette A violet enamel **ground** introduced at Sèvres in 1757.

Violeteers A vessel intended to hold herbs or petals.

Vitrifiable colours Coloured **enamels** which become fixed and glassy when fired.

Waster A deformed pot rejected by the factory.

Wreathing Spiral throwing marks following the contours of a vessel.

Wucai The "five-coloured" Chinese palette developed in the Ming dynasty; contains **underglaze** cobalt blue, with iron-red, turquoise, yellow and green **enamels**.

Yao-ware Wares from Chinese kilns.

Yingqing One of the earliest forms of Chinese porcelain. Meaning "cloudy" or "shadow blue", it was made in the Song and Yuan periods and features a translucent, off-white body with a blue-tinged glaze. Often decorated with carved or moulded designs.

Yueh yao A type of green-glazed Chinese **stoneware**, produced at Yueh Chou in Shensi province during the T'ang dynasty. A forerunner of **celadon** wares.

BIBLIOGRAPHY

GENERAL

Atterbury, Paul, *History of Porcelain*, London, 1982

Berges, Ruth, *From Gold to Porcelain; the Art of Porcelain and Faïence*, New York, 1963

Cushion, John, *Porcelain*, London, 1973

Charleston, Robert, Ed., *World Ceramics*, London, 1981

Fleming, John, and Honour, Hugh, *The Penguin Dictionary of the Decorative Arts*, London, 1977

Honey, W.B., *The Art of the Potter*, London 1980
Ceramic Art from the End of the Middle Ages to about 1815 (2 Vols), London, 1952

Miller, Judith and Martin, Ed., *Understanding Antiques*, London, 1989, published in the US as *Miller's World Encyclopedia of Antiques*

Morley-Fletcher, Hugo, Ed., *Techniques of the World's Great Masters of Pottery and Ceramics*, Oxford, 1984

Savage, George, *Porcelain through the Ages*, London, 1954

Sotheby's *Concise Encyclopedia of Porcelain*, London, 1990

ORIENTAL

Beurdeley, M., and Raindre, G, *Qing Porcelain: Famille Verte, Famille Rose*, London, 1987

Carswell, John, *Chinese Blue and White and its Impact on the Western World*, Chicago, 1985

Garner, Sir Henry, *Oriental Blue and White*, London 1970

Godden, G.A., *Oriental Export Market Porcelains*, London, 1979

Honey, W.B., *The Ceramic Art of China and Other Countries of the Far East*, London, 1945

Howard, D.S., *Chinese Armorial Porcelain*, London, 1974 and Ayers, J., *China for the West*, London, 1974

Jenyns, Soame, *Ming Pottery and Porcelain*, London, 1953
Later Chinese Porcelain, London, 1971
Japanese Porcelain, London, 1985

Jorg, C.J.A., *Porcelain and the Dutch China Trade*, The Hague, 1982

Kerr, R., *Chinese Ceramics: Porcelain of the Qing Dynasty 1664 - 1911*, London, 1986

Kwan, S., *Imperial Porcelain of the late Qing*, Hong Kong, 1983

Lunsingh Scheurleer, D.F., *Chinese Export Porcelain, Chine de Commande*, English translation, London, 1974

Medley, Margaret, *The Art of the Chinese Potter*, Oxford 1981

Munsterberg, Hugo, *The Ceramic Art of Japan*, New York, 1964

Reichel, Friedrich, *Early Japanese Porcelain*, London, 1981

Sato, M., *Chinese Ceramics, a Short History*, New York, 1981

EUROPEAN

Bellaigue, Geoffrey de, *Sèvres Porcelain from the Royal Collection*, London, 1979
Sèvres Porcelain in the Collection of Her Majesty the Queen: the Louis XVI Service, Cambridge, 1986

Brunet, Marcelle, and Preaud, T., *Sèvres. Des Origines à nos Jours*, Paris, 1978

Dauterman, C. Christian, *Sèvres*, New York, 1969
Sèvres Porcelain: Makers and Marks of the 18th Century, New York, 1986

Fay-Halle, Antoinette, and Mundt, Barbara, *Nineteenth Century European Porcelain*, London, 1983

Frothingham, Alice Wilson, *Capodimonte and Buen Retiro Porcelains, Period of Charles III*, New York, 1955

Garnier, Edouard, *The Soft Porcelain of Sèvres*, London, 1988

Hayward, John F., *Viennese Porcelain of the du Paquier Period*, London, 1952

Honey, W.B., *Dresden China*, London, 1934
French Porcelain of the 18th Century, London, 1950
European Ceramic Art, London, 1959

Kingery, W.D., and Vandiver, P.B., *Ceramic Masterpieces*, New York, 1986

Lane, Arthur, *Italian Porcelain*, London, 1954

Menzhausen, Ingelore, *Early Meissen Porcelain in Dresden*, London, 1990

Morley-Fletcher, Hugo, *Meissen*, London, 1971

Preaud, Tamamra, and Antoinette Fay-Halle, *Porcelaines de Vincennes, les Origines de Sèvres*, Paris, 1977

Ruckert, Rainer, *Meissener Porzellan, 1710 – 1810*, Munich, 1966 Franz Anton Bustelli, Munich, 1963

Savage, George, *Seventeenth and Eighteenth Century French Porcelain*, London, 1960
18th Century German Porcelain, London, 1958

Saville, Rosalind, *Sèvres Porcelain*, London, 1980

Tilmans, Emile, *Porcelaines de France*, Paris, 1954

BRITISH

Adams, E., *Chelsea Porcelain*, London, 1987

and Redstone, D., *Bow Porcelain*, London, 1981

Atterbury, P., and Batkin, M., *The Dictionary of Minton*, Woodbridge, 1990

Barrett, Franklin A., *Worcester Porcelain*, London, 1953

Caughley and Coalport Porcelain, Leigh-on-Sea, 1951

Worcester Porcelain and Lund's Bristol, London, 1966

and Thorpe, A.L., *Derby Porcelain*, London, 1971

Boney, Knowles, *Liverpool Porcelain*, London, 1957

Richard Chaffers, Liverpool, 1960

Bradshaw, Peter, *18th Century English Porcelain Figures*, Woodbridge, 1981

Derby Porcelain Figures, London, 1990

Charleston, R.J., Ed., *English Porcelain 1745 - 1850*, London, 1965

Cox, A. and A., *Rockingham Pottery and Porcelain*, London, 1983

Dixon, J.L., *English Porcelain of the Eighteenth Century*, London, 1953

Godden, G.A., *Eighteenth-Century English Porcelain*, London, 1985

Victorian Porcelain, London, 1961

British Porcelain: an Illustrated Guide, London, 1974

Encyclopaedia of English Porcelain Manufacturers, London, 1988

Pottery and Porcelain of the First Period, 1793 - 1850, London, 1968 Ed.,

Staffordshire Porcelain, London, 1983

Coalport and Coalbrookdale Porcelains, Woodbridge, 1981

Chamberlain Worcester Porcelain, London, 1982

Godden, G.A. and T. and Lockett, *Davenport Pottery and Porcelain*, London, 1989

Hillier, Bevis, *Pottery and Porcelain, 1700 - 1914*, London, 1968

Honey, W.B., *Old English Porcelain*, London, 1977

Hughes, Bernard and Therle, *English Porcelain and Bone China, 1743 - 1850*, New York, 1955

Jones, A.E., and Leslie, Sir Joseph, *Swansea Porcelain Shapes and Decoration*, Cowbridge, 1988

Lane, Arthur, *English Porcelain Figures of the Eighteenth Century*, London, 1961

Legge, Margaret, *Flowers and Fables. A Survey of Chelsea Porcelain, 1745 - 1769*, Melbourne, 1984

Mackenna, F. Severene, *18th Century English Porcelain*, Leigh-on-Sea, 1970

Cookworthy's Plymouth and Bristol Porcelain, Leigh-on-Sea, 1947

Champion's Bristol Porcelain, Leigh-on-Sea, 1947

Mankowitz, Wolf, and R.G. Haggar, *Concise Encyclopaedia of English Pottery and Porcelain*, London, 1968

Miller and Bertoud, *An Anthology of British Teapots*, London, 1985

Morton Nance, E., *The Pottery and Porcelain of Swansea and Nantgarw*, London, 1942

Murdoch, John, *Painters in the Derby China Works*, London, 1987

Sandon, H., *Royal Worcester Porcelain*, London, 1973

Flight & Barr Worcester Porcelain, Woodbridge, 1978

Savage, George, *Eighteenth Century English Porcelain*, London, 1951

English Pottery and Porcelain, New York, 1961

Stringer, G.E., *New Hall Porcelain*, London, 1949

Twitchet, John, *Derby Porcelain*, London, 1980

Watney, B.M., *English Blue & White Porcelain of the 18th Century*, London, 1973

Longton Hall Porcelain, London, 1957

Whiter, L., *Spode,* London, 1970

Williams-Woods, Cyril, *English Transfer-Printed Pottery and Porcelain*, London, 1981

AMERICAN

Barber, Edwin Atlee, T*he Pottery and Porcelains of the United States and Marks of American Potters*, New York, 1977

Barret, Richard Carter, *Bennington Pottery and Porcelain*, New York, 1958

Denker, Ellen and Bert, *North American Pottery and Porcelain*, Pittstown, 1985

Frelinghuysen, Alice Cooney, *American Porcelain Factory, 1770 - 1772*, New York, 1989

Hood, Graham, *Bonnin and Morris of Philadelphia - The First American Porcelain Factory, 1770 -1772*, Chapel Hill, 1972

Klamkin, M., *American Patriotic and Political China*, New York, 1973

Lehner, L., *The Complete book of American Kitchen and Dinner Wares*, Des Moins, 1980

Schwartz, M.D., and Wolf. R., *A History of American Art Porcelain*, New York, 1967

Spargo, J., *Early American Pottery and China*, New York, 1974

INDEX

PICTURE CREDITS AND ACKNOWLEDGMENTS

The publishers would like to thank the following auction houses, museums, dealers, collectors and other sources for kindly supplying pictures for use in this book.

1 SL; 3 SL; 10l CL; 10r SL; 11t CG;11b SL; 12l SL; 12rt SG; 12rb SG; 13 CL;16 SL; 20 SL; 21(x3) SL; 22 SL; 23(x4) SL; 24 SL; 25(x4) SL; 26 SL; 27lt SL; 27lc CL; 27lb SL; 27rt CL; 27rb SL; 28 SL;29lt SL; 29lb CL; 29rt SL; 29rc SL; 29rb CL; 30t SG; 30b CL; 31lt SL; 31lb SL; 31rt CNY; 31rc CNY; 31rb SL; 32 VA; 331 SL; 33rt SL; 33rc VA; 33rb VA; 34 SL; 35(x2) SL; 36(x2) SL; 37(x3) SL; 38(x2) SL; 39(x3) SL; 40t SL; 40rb SC; 48 SL; 49(x2) SL; 50 SL; 51rt SL; 51rb SL; 52 SL; 53(x5) SL; 54 SL;55lt SL; 55lb SZ; 55r(x3) SL; 56 SL; 57(x3) SL; 58 SL; 59(x5) SL; 60 SG; 61(x4) SL; 62 SL; 63l SNY; 63r SL; 64 SL; 65(x2) SL; 66 SL; 67l CL; 67r SZ; 68 SZ; 69(x4) SL; 70 SL; 71(x2) SL; 72 SL; 73l SNY; 73rt SL; 73rb SNY; 74 SL; 75l SNY; 76 SL; 77(x3) SL; 78 SL; 79(x4) SNY; 80 SL; 81(x3) SL; 82 SL; 83(x2)SL; 84 SL; 85 SL; 86 SL; 87 SL; 88(x2) SL; 89(x3) SL; 90 SL; 96 SL; 97(x2) SL; 98t SL; 98b SNY; 99 SL; 100 SL; 101lt SL; 101lb SL; 10lrt SNY; 101rb CL; 102t SL; 102b CL; 103t SL; 103b SL; 104 SL; 105lt CL; 105lb SL; 105rt SL; 105rc SL;105rb CL; 106 SL; 107(x3) SL; 108 CL; 109(x3) CL; 110 SL; 111l SM; 111rt CL; 111rb SL; 112 SL; 112l PC; 113rt SL; 113rb PC; 114t SL; 114b CL; 115l SL; 115rt SL; 115rb SL; 116 SL; 117lt SL; 117lb CNY; 117r SL; 118 SL; 119lt SL; 119lb SL; 119rt CL; 119rb CL; 120 SL; 121l SL; 121rt SL; 121rb SL; 122 CNY; 123lt SL; 123lb SL; 123r SL; 124 SL; 125(x3) SL; 126 CNY; 127l(x2) SL; 127rt PC; 127rb SL; 128 PC; 129lt,lc PC; 129lb PC; 129rt PC; 129rb SL; 130 SL; 131l(x2) CBM; 131rt NT; 131rb SL; 132 M; 133l(x2) M; 133rt M; 133rb SL; 134 SL; 135l(x2) SL; 135rt SL; 135r M; 135rb SNY; 136 SL; 137(x3) SL; 138 SNY; 139l(x3) SL; 139rt SNY; 139b SL; 140 SL; 141(x4) SL; 142 CL; 143l, rt PC; 143rb SL; 150t SL; 150b SL; 151(x2) SL; 152 SL; 153l SL; 153rt SL; 153rb JPGN; 154 SG; 155l(x2) SG;155rt SL; 155rb CL; 156 CL; 157lt SZ; 157b SG; 157rt SNY; 157rb SL; 158 BM; 160 Phil; 161 MM; 162 SNY; 163 SNY; 164 SI; 165 SNY; 166 SL; 167(x3) SL; 168lt SL; 168lb SL; 168r SL; 169(x5) SL; 170l&r SL; 171(x4) SL; 172(x3) SL; 173(x4) SL; 174t&b SL; 175(x4) SL.

KEY
b bottom, c centre, l left, r right, t top

BM	Brooklyn Museum, New York		Library
CBM	City of Bristol Museum and Art Gallery	PC	Private Collection
CG	Christie's, Geneva	Phil	Philadelphia Museum of Art
CL	Christie's, London	SG	Sotheby's, Geneva
CNY	Christie's, New York	SI	Skinner Inc, Boston
JPGM	J. Paul Getty Museum	SL	Sotheby's, London
M	Mercury Antiques	SM	Sotheby's, Monaco
MM	Metropolitan Museum of Art, New York	SNY	Sotheby's, New York
NT	National Trust Photo	SZ	Sotheby's, Zurich
		VA	Victoria and Albert Museum

Special thanks are due to Eric Knowles and Mrs L.Richards for their generous help in the presentation of this book, and to Nicholas Dawes, who contributed to the American section. The publisher would also like to thank Christopher Spencer for his help in updating this edition.